ROUTE 66 *Remembered*

Michael Karl Witzel

MBI Publishing Company

First published in 1996 by MBI Publishing Company, 729 Prospect Avenue, PO Box 1, Osceola, WI 54020-0001 USA

MBI Publishing Company books are also available at discounts in bulk quantity for industrial or sales-promotional use. For details write to Special Sales Manager at Motorbooks International Wholesalers & Distributors, 729 Prospect Avenue, PO Box 1, Osceola, WI 54020-0001 USA.

Library of Congress Cataloging-in-Publication Data
Witzel, Michael Karl
    Route 66 remembered / Michael Karl Witzel.
      p. cm.
    Includes index.
    ISBN 0-7603-0114-X (casebound: alk. paper)
    1. United States Highway 66—History. 2. United
    States Highway 66—History—Pictorial works. 3.
    Automobile travel—United States—History.
    4. Automobile travel—United States—History—
Pictorial works. I. Title.
HE356.U55W58 1996
388.1'0973—dc20   95-47984

On the front cover: Main image: Route 66 curved and rolled through eight states, three time zones, and numerous elevation changes as it meandered its way from Chicago to Los Angeles. This postcard from the 1940s depicts Tijeras Canyon in New Mexico. **Inset:** A collage of Route 66 images recalls the days of cheap gas, personal service, and carefree travel. *Author*

On the frontispiece: Heading towards Miami, Oklahoma, from the Brush Creek Bridge in Riverton, Kansas, white Route 66 shields have been painted on the road surface to guide those in search of the old alignment. New asphalt has been laid as well, making easy driving for all those in search of back-road bliss. Baxter Springs, Kansas. *Author*

On the title page: The Wigwam Village in San Bernardino, California, offered the weary traveler the chance to "sleep in a teepee!" Many of Route 66's roadside establishments reflected the history and folklore of the surrounding regions. *Preziosi Postcards*

On the back cover: Top: Roadside stops like the Big Arrows Trading Post in Houck, Arizona, were the convenience stores of the era. Such shops gave the motorist a chance to fuel his car, fill his stomach, and empty his wallet. *Courtesy Chuck Sturm*
Center: Route 66 travel guide cover. "America's Main Street" offered a quick path to the West Coast but was also a vacation destination in and of itself.
Bottom: Countless small privately-owned motels dotted Route 66's length. They offered a comfortable break from the road in the days before Best Western and other corporate giants controlled the roadside. *Author*

Printed in Hong Kong

Contents

Dedication

This book is dedicated to the four-wheeled, internal combustion conveyance that became my very first motorcar: a dark azure, second-hand, two-door, 1967 model Chevrolet Malibu Coupe equipped with a 283-cubic-inch V-8 engine, an automatic transmission that jerked when you shifted into reverse, air-conditioning that blew only slightly cool air, a Delco AM radio that pulled in mostly static, vinyl split-bench seats that were cold in the winter and sweaty in the summer, and a front window seal that leaked during heavy rains. For $800 it wasn't the perfect motoring machine, but it was all mine—providing the freedom to explore the open road and discover for myself the magic and wonders that were out there, somewhere . . . beyond the distant vanishing point, over the approaching hill, or waiting . . . just around the next bend.

Acknowledgments

Without the input and assistance of Paul Taylor, editor of Route 66 Magazine, this publication would have been stuck on the side of the highway. A heartfelt thank you to all of the individuals who shared their personal "Mother Road" memories, including Ralph Bay, Allen Bell, Jay Black, Bea Bragg, Terri Cleeland, David Cole, James Cook, Glen Driskill, Ken Greenburg, Rebecca Rockwood Hill, John Houghtaling, Mildred "Skeeter" Kobzeff, Gordon Kornblith, Richard McDonald, Joe Morrow, Mildred Birdsell Pattschull, Clare Patterson, Jr., Mabel Richards Phillips, Terri Ryburn-LaMonte, Bill Stevens, and Buz Waldmire. Further appreciation is extended to all of the photographers, artists, archives, and corporations that supplied images or information, most notably: A & W Restaurants, Inc.; Airstream, Inc.; the American Automobile Manufacturer's Association; the American Petroleum Institute; John Baeder; Kent Bash; Bob Boze Bell; Bennett Pump Company; Chevron Corporation; the General Motors Media Archives; the General Stamping and Manufacturing Company; Gilbarco, Inc.; Shellee Graham; Janice Griffith of the Old Trails Museum; Diane Hamilton; Dan Harlow; the Henry Ford Museum & Greenfield Village; Joan Johnson of Circa Research and Reference; Library of Congress; Jerry McClanahan; Mid-America Designs; the National Archives; Clare Patterson, Jr.; Personality Photos, Inc.; James Reed of the Rogers County Historical Society; Jim Ross; Keith Sculle; the Security Pacific Historical Photograph Collection; Phillips Petroleum Archives; Shell Oil Company; Steak n Shake, Inc.; Texas Pig Stands, Inc.; Tokheim Corporation; University of Louisville; D. Jeanene Tiner; Robert Waldmire; June Wian; Barry Williams of the American Streetscape Society; and Gabriele Witzel. Kudos to memorabilia collectors Carl Christiansen, Hugh Clarke, John Hutinett, Jerry Keyser, Sr., Richard McLay, Don Preziosi, Chuck Sturm, Bill Thomas, and Warren Winthrop. Finally, a personal acknowledgment is reserved for my wife, Gyvel Young-Witzel—a pedestrian who has permanently hung up her Route 66 walking shoes in favor of an automotive seat (and its relative safety). Good travels to all!

Foreword

After showman and circus owner Phineas Taylor Barnum opened his side show of human oddities, folks paused at length to look upon his bizarre attraction. Barnum, aware that the delay was causing long lines of potential, but impatient, customers, placed a brightly lettered sign over a doorway at the far end of the tent; "This way to the Great Egress" it proclaimed. Curious onlookers hurried forward to examine the mysterious and wondrous Egress. What they saw when they passed through the portal was the outside of the tent, for, as Webster tells us, "egress" means way out, place of going out, or exit.

To many folks, an interstate exit sign that points the way to Route 66 is like that egress. It's the direction to just another road, they conclude. A way to nothing wondrous—an exit—just a place of going out.

In contrast, people who have discovered and rediscovered the road at the end of that exit, talk of their experiences on the old asphalt and concrete trail in terms of endearment, using words the likes of "nostalgic" and "magical."

To novelist John Steinbeck, Route 66 was The Mother Road, the road of flight, and the glory road to the land of Second Chance.

To songwriter Bobby Troup, it was "My way . . . the highway that's the best." It was the highway of kicks.

To architect Frank Lloyd Wright, it was the chute of a tilting continent, on which everything loose seemed to be sliding into Southern California.

And to travel agencies, it was the chosen thoroughfare of the discriminating American tourist.

Nobody could possibly guess how many Americans—from the Oakies, Arkies, and Texies, to the flower children—would consider Route 66 to be, first and foremost, an invitation for an extended stroll.

The nation first became aware of U.S. Highway 66 when the 1928 International Transcontinental Foot Marathon (affectionately known as the Bunion Derby) followed all of 66.

Three decades later, for a fee of $1,500, Pete McDonald walked on stilts from New York City to Los Angeles, a distance of 3,250 miles. From Chicago, the way west was Route 66. Pete was neither the first nor the last to place America's Main Street in the public eye: wild, weird, and wondrous celebrants were to follow.

Hobo Dick Zimmerman routinely walked Route 66 from California to Michigan pushing a wheelbarrow, to visit his 101-year-old mother. Dick was 78.

Another student of perambulating the old highway was "Shopping Cart" Dougherty, who, sporting a white beard and turban, traveled 9 to 16 miles a day on Route 66 with all his worldly possessions in a shopping cart.

Shopping Cart and Hobo Dick weren't the most unusual challengers and celebrants of the Mother Road. High school baton twirlers marched along Old 66 setting dubious records.

In 1972, John Ball, a 45-year-old South African, jogged from California to Chicago on Route 66, and then on to the East Coast. The journey took 54 days.

The 1920s and 1930s saw desperadoes and bootleggers the likes of John Dillinger, Al Capone, and Bugs Moran lurching down Old 66, the escape route. Occasionally, the Associated Press warned travelers of the dangers of "the criminally few who mix with the tourist throng."

National magazines called 66 "America's Worst Speed Trap," naming the tiny hamlets where cops and judges had their palms outstretched. The American Automobile Association reported towns you should avoid, or else prepare to sweeten the police treasury.

For a six-year-old child traveling with his parents in a brand new 1937 Chevy, Route 66 is memories of a canvas water bag on the front bumper, buying maple syrup at Funks Grove, Illinois, crossing the Chain of Rocks Bridge on the Mississippi River, visiting Meramec Caverns in Missouri, and listening to Dad read aloud every single Burma-Shave sign encountered along the road. I don't recall if my father used the product or not, but I do remember that his favorite verse was "Don't stick your elbow out too far/It might go home in another car." Since I always had my arm out the window, that was probably a personal message for me.

Today, with my own family, that same highway becomes more and more special with each journey. Old landmarks appear from the crest of a hill . . . a gas station or diner now closed, but still, memories flicker.

The two-laner turns, rises, and twists its way across the country. Hundreds and hundreds of drivable miles are still out there. Some of the road echoes to that familiar thump-ah, thump-ah, thump-ah rhythm as the tires bounce over separations in the WPA concrete slabs. But, in stark contrast, many miles of the old road have a surface more pleasant to drive than some parts of the interstates.

Although Route 66 is somewhat hidden in the shadows of the superhighways, progress does not necessarily conquer all. Diners and roadside attractions are still out there. Some are only gaunt images of their former selves, while others have been restored and reopened.

A glance through the pages of this book evokes memories of those businesses that once lined that scenic, narrow, two-lane, wavy old road. Author Michael Karl Witzel awakens the nostalgic era when life was less complex, when a rural economy was still dominant, when the jukebox in the back room of a mom-and-pop diner blared out "Good Night Irene," a cup of coffee cost a nickel, and there was more action in the back seat of a car at the drive-in movie than on the screen.

—Paul Taylor, publisher *Route 66 Magazine*, Laughlin, Nevada

Take a Drive Along America's Main Street

chapter one

Were we really in the country? If so, where was it? The road was bordered with big hoardings, not presenting a flat surface or even painted in such a way as to create an illusion of reality, but complicated with depth and perspective; that is, made like a stage-setting with converging wings, and with figures cut out from wood in the open space in between, and at nightfall the whole thing was illuminated with rows of electrical light at top and bottom. Behind these enormous structures there may perhaps have been what passes for the country hereabouts.

—Georges Duhamel, America the Menace: Scenes From the Life of the Future, 1931

Tourist Traps:
Attractions Along the Road

*Throughout the Roar*ing Twenties and straight on up to the 1960s, the roadsides along Route 66 jumped with an eclectic mix of attractions. Back then, America's Main Street was the nation's premier ride—a two-lane roller coaster of thrills that rambled through eight states and three time zones. All along the miles of the "linear midway," a diversity of car commerce combined services motorists required with the entertainment they desired.

With a full tank of fuel, a good night's snooze, and a belly filled with road food—motorized attendees of the

During the golden age of the highway, animal attractions along the road were intense by today's standards. With less concern over crowded and inhumane conditions, proprietors interested more in a fast buck than the preservation of nature established all sorts of outlandish zoos and curiosity shows. In Two Guns, Arizona, the legend of an Indian massacre where Apaches killed 40 Navajo men, women, and children provided the perfect story to promote the local tourist trade. Intrigued by the idea of an "Apache Death Cave," Route 66 travelers wheeled in to get their macabre kicks. *Courtesy Paul Taylor*

left
Amid the rabble of souvenir shops vying for attention along the old route, Joseph Joe's Big Indian Store was once an able contender. Capitalizing on the imagery of the native American (in an era when no one thought twice about exploiting stereotypes), it was a roadside curiosity shop that more than piqued the interest of the vacationer motoring down Route 66. Winslow, Arizona, circa 1983. *Jerry McClanahan ©1995*

11

roadside carnival pushed down on the accelerator to bring on the wonders. Near the highway's western limit in the city of Los Angeles, wheeling past a barbecue stand constructed like an immense pig was an everyday occurrence. Out there, short-order food shacks were shaped like giant toads and juice joints bloated up as over-sized oranges.

At the outskirts of town where traffic dwindled, automobile ownership allowed day-trippers to experience the full glory of 66. Beneath the gaping grin of a life-size dinosaur, couples could picnic without care. When a long day of explorations were concluded, it was all the rage to catch 40 winks inside an Indian wigwam, refill one's gas tank at a petrified-wood service station, or dine on a corned-beef sandwich inside the penthouse of a gigantic shoe. Route 66 held an endless array of surprises!

With turning a profit of paramount importance, the roadside businesses lining the highway employed every trick they could think of to lure motorists. They had no alternative: When automobile ownership during the teens and 1920s rose to

The Roadside Delight Called Spooklight

"Governed by seemingly magical properties, it waltzes through mesquite groves and leaps over fences, sometimes bouncing right off passing automobiles. . . ."

Since 1886, mysterious orbs of light have been bobbing up and down in the woods of northeastern Oklahoma. The Quapaw Indians caught first glimpse of these fluttering flashes, and later, residents of the town taking their name spied them as well. Local landowners nicknamed the glow "Spooklight" and began to weave tales of mystery and imagination to explain its origin. Today—the eerie phenomenon is an established Route 66 attraction, drawing throngs of curiosity-seekers to the twisting road dubbed "Devil's Promenade."

Seen mostly in July during overcast skies, the Spooklight is routinely reported as a bright, yellow-white sphere of light—one that occasionally transforms into a fiery red. Originating as a single globe of energy, it has been known to divide at will and form two bouncing blobs, each exhibiting its own directional agenda and duration. Governed by seemingly magical properties, it waltzes through mesquite groves and leaps over fences, sometimes bouncing right off passing automobiles (in one rare occurrence it entered the passenger compartment through an open window). When approached, it disappears, when chased, it eludes.

Witnesses have often described Spooklight's mimicry of a searchlight, lending credence to the skeptic's standard explanation of the anomaly. As far back as the 1920s, practical thinkers have fingered the motorcar as the most culpable suspect, describing how refracted light shone from vehicle headlamps on 66 could be the only logical source for the illumination. However, old timers vehemently dismiss the theory since many witnessed the enigmatic glow long before there were any roads or the town of Quapaw.

Some claim the puzzling lights have been around since the beginning of time. As far back as the days of the clipper ships, Mediterranean seamen were perplexed by the mercurial flames hovering about their masts. Deckhands christened the odd glow "St. Elmo's Fire"—a derivation of St. Erasmus, the patron saint of sailors. In other countries, the peculiar phenomenon has been affectionately referred to as "spunkie," "jack-o'-lantern," and "will-o'-the-wisp." In most instances, rotting tree stumps and humid marshes are the recognized haunts for this so-called *ignis fatuus* (from the Latin, meaning foolish fire).

In Oklahoma, regional folklore endeavors to demystify the conundrum with an "old" Indian tale. According to legend, a brave was prematurely relieved of his head during a domestic argument. His disgruntled spouse hid the severed head somewhere among the trees, north of Miami, Oklahoma. Spooklight simply became the earthly manifestation of his spirit—doomed to an eternal search for his misplaced head.

Nevertheless, none of these yarns formed a scientific hypothesis to explain the spectacle. So, during the 1940s, a concerted effort was initiated by the U.S. Corps of Engineers to debunk the fallacies and find the truth. As WWII raged on, they descended on northeastern Ottawa County and organized a research camp. For almost a month they explored caves, analyzed mineral deposits, sifted streams, and studied road alignments. Despite a thorough examination, the unpredictable conduct of the bizarre lights could not be reckoned with physical laws! Decades later, the "Unsolved Mysteries" television series mounted its own investigation. Once again, no concrete answers were found.

Even so, some concluded that certain geological events—combined with just the right temperature and atmospheric conditions—triggered outbreaks of these fickle flames. A spontaneous combustion of gases was given as the most logical cause. Others cited the theoretical existence of ball lightning, a specialized form of ionized gas known as "plasma" that, given the right parameters, can form at will. Like the tornado, there's no predicting when it will occur, where it will go, and how long it will last. The only absolute: The lucky few who see it will gaze with child-like wonder and amazement.

And luck has become a prerequisite, since the wily Spooklight has shifted its location over the years. Without rhyme or reason, it has steadily drifted farther and farther to the northeast, almost to the state line of Kansas. Fortunately, anticipation and a sense of adventure are more important to the two-lane travelers who come to sneak a peek at this enigmatic pixie. After all, the romantic idea of nature's mystery—something that defies our comprehension and can never be bought, sold, or bottled for sale at a souvenir stand—is what makes the quest unique. That's the real appeal of Quapaw's Spooklight. As long as there are still occasional sightings of those little white lights that "go bump in the night," it always will be.

Right off of old Route 66 in Quapaw, Oklahoma, the twisting stretch of road known as Devil's Promenade has, until recently, been the primary point for sighting the elusive Spooklight. Sightings reported during the mid-1990s have indicated that the phenomenon is now moving steadily to the northeast—right across the Kansas state line. Still, there is no way to predict when and where the next manifestation of Spooklight will occur. Quapaw, Oklahoma. *Special-Effects Recreation by Author*

become secondary only to shelter and clothing—the trading climate along America's roadsides became increasingly competitive. As a steady influx of new drivers turned a dirt artery into a transcontinental corridor, new types of industries emerged to accommodate the flow.

Before too long, services that catered to the motor vehicle were duplicated in vast numbers. With the corresponding rise in Route 66 advertisers vying for attention, the raft of billboards and snipe signs common to early motor trails became impotent. At what used to be a quiet country crossroads, Chuck's Chicken Shack now had to contend with a self-contained dining car across the street and a cafeteria on the corner. As travelers sped past with no end in sight, the friendly neighborhood filling station suddenly found itself in competition with two additional "service" stations and a lubritorium on the very same block!

The need to achieve greater visibility—and a unique hook—increased. To break through the visual cacophony, some Route 66 entrepreneurs decided to erect bigger and more brightly lit signs. Others took the craft of outdoor advertising to a new level with neon-lit creations of pressed steel and glass tubing. Born of the merchant's imagination, roadside statues made of plaster and lath were used to attract the motorist's ever-decreasing attention. A few businesses that depended directly on the car for business decided to blend both their building and billboard by utilizing the "programmatic" themes so popular on the coast. By

In June 1929, "Happy" Lou Phillips and his partner "Lucky" Jimmy Parker strapped on a pair of roller skates and rolled across America. From Washington, D.C., to San Francisco, California, they skated all the way—supporting themselves by selling their photographs, doing some vaudeville shows, and peddling newspapers in the cities they passed through. They followed Route 66 through Arizona and into California and, according to a story in the Williams (Arizona) News, explained that "[when] we travel on the roads that are not concreted, we keep the skates on and walk on them. On dirt roads, we go from 20 to 55 miles a day, but on concrete roads we make 75 miles a day." Their trip ultimately took them through 17 states and a distance of 4,563 miles! *Courtesy Hugh Clarke via Terri Cleeland*

"The Chain of Rocks Bridge," Highway 66 over Mississippi River near St. Louis, Mo.

BL 76

K 150

The Chain of Rocks bridge was once the principle means for Route 66 motorists to get across the Mississippi River. About halfway across the span, a distinct curve was an integral part of the unique, steel-truss design. Today, the aging bridge has been retired and cannot be accessed from the Missouri side of the river. However, the road (right behind the chain-link fence on Riverfront Road, south of Interstate 270) can still be explored on foot. Near St. Louis, Missouri. *Courtesy Jerry Keyser*

copying the whimsical forms of animals or objects and incorporating them into their buildings, operators blended billboards with architecture. By the time construction crews were laying concrete along the final miles of Highway 66, an exciting roster of restaurants, gas stations, tourist courts, souvenir stands, and other recreational hideaways were entertaining the travelers with architectural theatrics. In Oklahoma,

a smiling blue whale splashed about in the waters near Catoosa. Just down the highway in Foyil, tourists were allowed to explore the inside of a multicolored totem pole. Meanwhile, the good folks in Texas slapped an oversized set of longhorns and a ten-gallon hat on just about everything. New Mexico traders adopted the Indian mystique, and in the stretch of road through Arizona the shapely saguaro became a predominant theme. By the time man orbited the Earth, Paul Bunyan had donned a space helmet (with hand-held missile) near Wilmington, Illinois!

As the rush to motorize changed America, the "Mother Road" became a bona fide destination in itself. Timid automobile owners who never dreamed of leaving the confines of their state took to the highway with great zeal—just to see how easy it was to travel long distances. Suddenly, the owners of roadside businesses began to realize that there was much more to making money along a busy thoroughfare than just renting out tourist cabins, pumping gas, or serving chili: When a traveler's needs were taken care of and they were ready to continue the journey, thoughts often turned to mementos of the trip. Everyone, it seemed, wanted a souvenir to show the folks back home—proof of exactly where they had been and the adventures they had experienced.

Unprepared for the rising demand, Route 66 operators learned first hand of the motorist's sentimental acquisitiveness: day in and day out, ash trays, towels, tableware, napkin holders, coffee cups, salt and pepper shakers, and anything else that could be carried off began to disappear. In an effort to discourage this depletion of operating equipment and to increase revenue, the idea of selling specialized souvenirs was seriously considered. Unsure of the territory, the trio of roadside services known as gas, food, and lodging were entering the retail world.

Between the towns of Rolla and Waynesville, Missouri, a four-lane length of Route 66 created the "deepest rock cut in the U.S." In the 1940s, the massive soil excavation was a road engineering achievement that allowed passengers inside automobiles to view a real roadside attraction without slowing down—or even leaving the comfort of their cars. *Courtesy Jerry Keyser*

The Chain of Rocks Bridge opened as a toll bridge for motor traffic in 1929. Linking the north side of St. Louis, Missouri, and the town of Mitchell on the Illinois side, it offered motorists a roadbed that was only 40 feet wide. In 1930, the St. Louis alignment of Route 66 was rerouted to avoid the bustling railroad and warehouse congestion and subsequently linked up with the Chain of Rocks. By the 1970s, the bridge was abandoned and visitors to and from St. Louis were rerouted to more modern spans. *Shellee Graham ©1995*

17

Of Speed Traps and Traffic Tickets

"Wide-eyed tourists out to view the wonders of America soon discovered that a revolving red light flashing in their rear view-mirror was one of the more unwelcome sights."

At the turn of the century, receiving a speeding ticket was more unlikely then being struck by lightning while fixing a flat. After all, no substantial traffic laws existed in the West until well after Ford introduced the Model T. As late as the 1930s, a dozen states had absolutely no speed limit at all! A few posted placards suggested a "safe and reasonable" rate, indirectly sanctioning motorists to put the "pedal to the metal."

Despite the lax attitudes, densely populated regions were attempting to regulate motoring's unbridled passions. In 1909, the city of Pittsburgh, Pennsylvania, set an example when they equipped their policemen with a secret weapon: the motorcycle. With a powerful V-twin engine and agility in heavy traffic, the Harley-Davidson police bike could catch up to even the speediest roadster! It didn't take long for other cities to notice. By the mid-1920s, over 2,500 towns were employing racy two-wheelers to nab traffic violators.

By the 1930s, being pulled over by a "motorcycle cop" and cited for excessive speed became a recognized risk for the car crowd. The minor trepidation sensed along the motor lanes soon grew to a panic: a few unscrupulous townships (along the well-traveled routes such as 66) calculated that the endless procession of cars cruising across their borders could be tapped as a lucrative source of revenue. Without bothering to build a motor court, restaurant, gas station, or even a tourist attraction, they proceeded to reap the road's bounty. All that was required to hook 'em was an overeager official in uniform . . . hidden behind a strategically placed billboard.

Wide-eyed tourists out to view the wonders of America soon discovered that a revolving red light flashing in their rear-view mirror was one of the more unwelcome sights. With their sirens wailing, helmets strapped tight, and ticket pads at the ready, the overzealous watchdogs of our nation's hinterlands introduced the unwary motorists to their most novel gambit: the "speed trap"! The so-called golden age of the automobile was beginning to show some tarnish.

To determine if a car was going too fast, patrolmen who were on the level usually timed a vehicle's movement between a set of marked reference points. The unfair officer casually eye-balled an approaching vehicle and determined by sight if it was exceeding the posted limits. In some cases, speed limits were left unposted at the outskirts, leaving motorists at a marked disadvantage and oblivious to the required reduction in speed. Disputing the accusations or denying to sign off on the traffic ticket wasn't recommended—after all, these were the days when no one questioned a policeman's authority.

With kids crying in the back seat, the wife growing impatient, and egg-salad turning rancid in the picnic basket, it was easy for country cops and judges to extract inflated fines from out-of-state vacationers. Far from home and eager to continue their journeys (waiting for a trial could often take up to two weeks), most "offenders" decided to cough up the extortion dough. With their wallets lightened and their blood pressure heightened, traffic scofflaws made a quick path past the city limits—muttering obscenities under their breath and vowing that they would never, ever pass this way again.

Eventually, word of the unsavory speed scam spread around, alerting other long-distance drivers to the dangers. Sympathetic journalists also taken in by the traps began to write revealing articles about their own experiences. Over the years, stories detailing the whereabouts of "America's Worst Speed Traps" appeared in *Argosy* magazine and a host of others. The American Automobile Association maintained a national reporting bureau as well, compiling a master list of municipalities responsible for the most flagrant abuses. Believe it or not, over half the trouble spots were identified along Route 66!

To everyone's approval, the speed trap phenomenon began to diminish during the 1960s, but never died out completely. As the interstate highway planners bypassed more and more villages with endless ribbons of freeway, the traditional methods—once used for generating honest cash flow—had to be reexamined. It was no longer economically viable for one-horse towns to repel the tourist just-passing-through with a rash of superfluous traffic citations!

For some communities, the change of heart occurred too late. America's motorized river of gold was now being rerouted, guided by steel guardrails and controlled by limited access and exit ramps. Whizzing along on the elevated superslab, the next generation of would-be speeders had fallen under the jurisdiction of the state highway patrolman. The inequitable era of the small town speed trap was finally over. Or was it?

The NEW All-Solid-State MOTORCYCLE RADIO from General Electric

Before two-way radios became technologically feasible and affordable for police departments, catching speeders and other scofflaws by automobile was difficult. Unable to radio ahead and alert additional cruisers, the police were impotent when it came to rum runners in souped-up hot rods. Unfortunately, the widespread use of the vacuum tube followed by the perfection of the transistor led to the development of inexpensive and efficient transceivers. By the end of the 1950s, municipalities all over America (and up and down Route 66) were putting the squeeze on speeders. *Courtesy General Electric via Preziosi Postcards*

At the wayside cafes, cashier stations doubled as display areas for knick-knacks. Colorful matchbooks emblazoned with whimsical captions, cartoons, and other advertisements became the staple item to give away free (when one purchased a cigar or pack of cigarettes). At dining tables, some restaurants slipped imprinted place-mats under the table-settings. Featuring facts and figures pertinent to the local area along with idealized reviews of the high-way's attractions, they were inexpensive give-aways to keep on hand. Of course, nothing reminded one of eating out away from home as much as a souvenir menu. Statues were cast, coins minted, glassware etched, and guidebooks printed.

For the majority of Route 66 operators, the linen picture postcard became the most cost-effective method to advertise a road-side business and get name recognition on a national level. When it was provided gratis, enthusiastic patrons were more than willing to provide the penny postage and to mail it off—sending home what amounted to nothing more than a personalized, direct-mailer to receptive friends and family. No amount of advertising could equal the hand-written testimonials describing attractions found along the "Great Diagonal Highway."

As pictures were examined on front porches in small-town America, kids marveled at the sight of their own road vanishing into the distance—tied like a string to a world of possibilities yet undiscovered. It was a world of travel that was opening up

Along Route 66 in Groom, Texas, the Britten U.S.A. water reservoir features one leg shorter than all the others. Locals like to think of it as promotion, but those driving by just think of it as another unusual sight along the American roadscape. Panhandle 66, Groom, Texas. *D. Jeanene Tiner ©1995*

19

In towns throughout the United States, a variety of automotive repair facilities, restaurants, retail stores, and chainsaw repair shops (in this case) have employed the services of "people attractors" to lure in the motorist and his money. Giant cow heads, cheeseburgers, mosquitoes, flamingos, mushrooms, plates of ribs, guns, and ice cream cones are frequent sights up on the rooftops. This fiberglass Paul Bunyan is only one of many statues available to the modern entrepreneur not afraid of a little showmanship. North service road (Route 66) of Interstate 44, Sullivan, Missouri. *Shellee Graham ©1995*

The Launching Pad Drive-In is one eatery that Route 66 motorists find difficult to speed past. Formerly known as the Dairy Delight, this restaurant's name was changed in 1965 during the space race frenzy. A local girl came up with a memorable moniker for the parking lot giant out front, officially kicking off the advertising career of the "Gemini Giant." The larger-than-life statue (28 feet tall) was manufactured by an advertising company in California and specially modified to reflect the rocketman motif. A few years ago, local high school kids took to stealing the 10-foot-long missile cradled in his arms, and now the practice has turned into an annoying—if not expensive—ritual. Wilmington, Illinois. *Shellee Graham ©1995*

Grand Canyon Caverns is an underground cave attraction that has really nothing in common with its famous namesake. Located about 200 miles from the real Grand Canyon between Seligman and Kingman, Arizona, it's a popular roadside stop for tourists making their way across the desert on the old cut of Arizona Highway 66. A huge statue of Tyrannosaurus Rex serves as the tourist magnet and an underground tour and gift shop the entertainment. East of Peach Springs, Arizona. *Shellee Graham ©1995*

to all: In the decade following World War II, the suspension of all gasoline rationing and the production of bigger, better motorcars equated to a renewed level of mobility. Young dreamers who did without were now coming of age and taking to the highways to make their own memories. Highway volume increased so much that by the close of the 1940s, the demand for sentimental sundries spurred a handful of hopefuls in Arizona and New Mexico to jump in with full-scale retail operations.

Before tourists could hide their wallets, savvy salesmen were recruiting the local Indian crafts people and scouring trade shows for desirable products. Itching to cash in on the coast-to-coast commuter, elaborate merchandising markets—or "trading posts" as they were called—were established at various points along Highway 66. The outskirts of major population centers in the Southwest got more than their fair share, followed by adjoining states and other regions in the Ozarks. In the postwar era, taking a trip down the Will Rogers Highway meant trading with the Indians.

For the vacationing family motoring out to view the wonder of the Painted Desert, trading posts were found to exhibit even more color. The fierce competition for customers ignited an endless duel to install the most saturated neon sign, construct the most colossal fantasy figure, or splash exteriors with the most garish paints. In most instances, all of the outside walls facing the highway became the canvas for a visual sales spiel. Three-foot-high lettering trumpeted an outfit's name as hanging sign boards (edged in jagged cuts) announced the collection of goods inside.

While the visual pulling power of the Geronimo trader had most of the nearby setups licked, one local competitor came up with a way to influence the customer hundreds of miles before they even crossed into the Grand Canyon State. James Taylor, operator of the Jackrabbit Trading Post, joined forces with Wayne Troutner (legendary owner of Winslow's Store for Men) and traveled Highway 66 on a all-out mission to advertise. Armed with a truckload of signs—bright yellow Jackrabbit signs—he plastered as much of the American roadside as possible with his namesake!

It was a hands-on approach to advertising that over the years fired up motorists' imaginations and developed an invaluable aura of mystery for his merchandising market. At the same time, it heightened the Jackrabbit's status as a Route 66 legend—fueling the interest of vacationers willing to go out and find it. One way or another, cars would eventually drive up to the Jackrabbit

MOTHER GOOSE PANTRY

During the 10-year span from 1925 through 1934, California led the way with programmatic architecture. The Mother Goose Pantry "restaurant in a shoe" was perhaps the most memorable of this design discipline, offering sit-down dining to customers inside of a replica brogue. Route 66 patrons of the late 1920s had the choice of consuming their lunch in the lower eating area of the shoe or taking the stairs to an elevated dining room. 1929 East Colorado Boulevard, Pasadena, California. *Preziosi Postcards*

Howdy Hank's was a Route 66 trading post that got its start as the Hopi Village. This whimsical character adorned the exterior wall and greeted customers in search of souvenirs. When Howdy Hank's changed ownership and was later reopened as Sitting Bull's Indian store, the future for this friendly wall painting was uncertain. By the time Sitting Bull ceased operations, the paint was already fading and beginning to peel. When a feed store took up residence and the walls were repainted, all evidence of the smiling cowpoke was hidden. Another of the unique sights along 66 had run out of time. Joseph City, Arizona, 1988. *Jerry McClanahan ©1995*

Trading Post. Painted in bold letters on a yellow slat billboard, a final exclamation greeted sojourners with a pithy "Here It Is." Perched atop the sign, a silhouette of an immense jackrabbit and a row of companion bunnies caught the eye of passing traffic. Of course, the three-foot-high composition jackrabbit (with yellow eyes) positioned at the front gate didn't hurt business. That was the real magnet for the kids.

In addition to memorable mascots and searing color schemes, most of the souvenir supershops borrowed extensively from Native American heritage. The connection became most obvious in their practical architecture: Influenced by the Iroquois style long house and the rectangular motifs of the Hopi pueblo, trading posts were typically long, low, flat-roofed structures constructed of cinder-block walls and finished

In Oklahoma, many closed portions of the old road may be traveled along the frontage of the new highway. While roadblocks, a lack of bridges, and removed sections of roadbed discourage any real long-distance exploring—the segments that do remain conjure up a sense of time and place unknown along the modern superhighway. Near Bristow, Oklahoma. *Author*

The Elusive Meteorite of Barringer's Crater

"Despite his inability to locate the mother of all space rocks . . . Barringer made believers out of the skeptics who ridiculed his earlier theories."

The biggest Route 66 attraction is not a building, not an animal farm, not a souvenir stand, nor a restaurant. It's a natural formation, an oversized hole in the ground known as Meteor Crater, located south of the old road between Flagstaff and Winslow in Leeup, Arizona. Created more than 49,000 years ago when prehistoric man was just beginning to experiment with the possibilities of the wheel, it has been a popular "roadside" attraction ever since.

While Indians roaming the region have recognized the landmark for well over 1,500 years (some have even linked it with their tribal customs and legends), early explorers of the American West formally "discovered" the gargantuan gash around 1871. White men hastily named it "Coon Butte" and just as recklessly began to propagate unfounded theories as to its origin. At first, all logical reasoning pointed to the possibility of volcanic activity. It was said that the violent release of subterranean steam and other gases blew the colossal cavity into creation.

However, most of these uninspired explanations were dismissed when Philadelphia mining engineer Daniel Moreau Barringer took possession of the crater in 1902. In the desert territory around the site, he discovered a profusion of metallic meteorites—ranging from pea-sized bits to shards larger than a marble. Concurrently, rare minerals such as coesite and stishovite were unearthed throughout the zone of impact. Convinced that an immense object from another world was the cause of these aberrations, he filed for a mining claim to explore the site.

For the next 25 years, he embarked on a relentless campaign of scientific study to prove that the crater was formed by the impact of a meteoric mass. He began his quest by searching for what he believed to be an immense ore body—a galactic treasure buried deep beneath the desert floor. If unearthed, it would be the largest (and most valuable) meteorite ever discovered by man. Taking into account the specimen's publicity value and importance in scientific circles, conservative estimations valued the find in excess of $1 billion.

Much to Barringer's chagrin, the task of ferreting out the whereabouts of the suspect "fragment" wasn't as simple a task as he had hoped. Erroneously, he had made the assumption that the space stone had fallen from the heavens on more or less a straight course. Because of this innocent miscalculation, his excavation at the center of the crater yielded nothing more exotic than dirt. Undaunted, Barringer and team continued prospecting—confounded by the disappointing progress of the drilling.

Eventually, Barringer came to the realization that the asteroid might have entered the Earth's atmosphere at a more acute angle. But if so, would it still have created the same kind of circular cavity? A simple experiment consisting of a rifle bullet fired into a patch of mud yielded the answer: Yes, high speed objects entering the soil from a shallow trajectory do produce impact craters with round characteristics. All this time, he was prospecting for the elusive hunk of iron at the wrong coordinates!

During the twilight of the 1940s, an imposing stone structure built by Daniel Moreau Barringer stood sentinel atop a nearby hill, about 1/2 mile east of the Route 66 junction with Meteor Crater Road (north of the present-day crater exit on Interstate 40). Although the view from this lookout was less-than-ideal, the castle-like monument was touted as the "Meteor Crater Observatory." Inside, a quarter allowed access to the narrow stairs that led to the top of a viewing tower. Up above, both young and old gazed at the wonders through a telescope! In the distance, one could see Meteor Crater all right—and on a clear day, even the jagged peaks of Moon Mountain (the highest point of the crater's blasted rim) were visible. But that was only part of the fun: During twilight, the nearby Painted Desert came alive with color. As coyotes yipped in celebration, the peaks of the San Francisco mountains bid farewell to the sun while the Hopi Mesas tucked themselves in for the night. Near Meteor Crater, Arizona. *Courtesy Paul Taylor*

With this new nugget of information, puzzling measurements began to make sense. Now, there was good reason for the horizontal rock formations on the south wall to be canted upwards 100 feet higher than outcroppings on the rim. In earnest, new drilling was initiated on the southeast side. When the bit seized up at a depth of 1,376 feet, there was renewed hope. Was it jammed between hard chunks of meteor? Barringer never found out. He had already spent $600,000 on the obsession and was forced to discontinue in 1929 when funds ran out.

Despite his inability to locate the mother of all space rocks, the undertaking proved to be a success. In the end, Barringer made believers out of the skeptics who ridiculed his earlier theories. He passed away that same year, canonized as the world's first person to demonstrate that large chunks of matter occasionally intersect the Earth's orbit . . . and slam right into it. But even more important, he gained respect for his hypothesis that

Meteor Crater remains a bona fide tourist attraction and oddity on old Route 66. It's a natural landmark that strikes to the very heart of human vulnerability and pulls the cosmic rug right out from under those who view it. For potential visitors traveling along 66 during the heyday, the idea of an immense meteor hole was reason enough to stop their cars. From Chicago to Santa Monica—and all points in between—tourists arrived by automobile to witness the results of nature's fury (and to buy a few mementos). Leeup, Arizona. *Courtesy Jerry Keyser and Guy Kudlemyer*

a gigantic nickel-iron asteroid zooming in from outer space at more than 100 times the velocity of a bullet tore out half a billion tons of rock from the Arizona plain.

Years later, additional expeditions aimed at finding the physical remnants of the main mass met with similar defeat. Only when sophisticated measuring devices employing electronic sensors were brought in did evidence of the giant meteorite surface. Ironically, 10 percent of the object was located under Meteor Crater's south rim—exactly where Daniel Moreau Barringer was forced to discontinue his search.

in stucco. Ornamentation and decoration were kept to a bare minimum.

Ten miles west of Winslow, Arizona, Ray Meany's fabulous Hopi House set the standard for architectural aesthetics. Made of adobe set in mud mortar, it was a design that featured exposed roof timbers, an exterior staircase, and a restrained application of flamboyant advertising. With most of the tourist markets along Highway 66 designed for maximum flash, Meany's multi-level trading complex was a tasteful exception to the rule.

Despite the rare operators who showed restraint, showmanship ruled the road: At Winslow's Big Indian Trading Post, a three-story representation of an angry, tomahawk

During the early 1920s, when portions of road that were to become Route 66 were yet unpaved, motorists passing through New Mexico could routinely view native architecture. In 1923, the village of Acoma, New Mexico, existed as one of the oldest inhabited pueblos in the United States. *National Archives*

wielding chief (sporting a feathered headdress and a full complement of war paint) nonchalantly rested his arm on a rooftop sign. Tepee Curios in Tucumcari, New Mexico, grafted one-half of a Plains Indian dwelling (outlined with neon tubing) onto its streetside facade. Car customers attracted by the curious sight entered through the pulled-back flap that led them to a standard-sized door opening.

In Lupton, the Tomahawk Trading Post billed itself as the last stop out of Arizona and took Indian weaponry to the extreme. In the parking lot, a massive sign depicting an idealized tomahawk loomed high above multiple lanes of gas pumps. In the "stone" portion of the giant ax, numerals were posted to alert all those zooming past of discount gasoline sold at "truckers' prices."

Inside the trading posts, the atmosphere often matched the excitement of the exterior. Everything under the desert sun was available for purchase. Jewelry was a mainstay, including handmade designs from Navajo and Zuni craftsmen. One could purchase elaborate squash-blossom necklaces, earrings, bracelets, strings of beads, belt-buckles—anything and everything that could hold a chunk of polished turquoise. The Big Arrow trading post in Houck, Arizona, even featured a line of "Squaw Dress Originals by Arlene!"

For the discriminating consumer, there were woven Indian blankets and rugs, tom-toms, belts, purses, and the ubiquitous

The Blue Whale used to be one of those Route 66 attractions that really packed 'em in. Hugh Davis built the whale for his wife, Zelta, and presented it to her as a wedding present in the early 1970s. Set in a spring-fed lake on their property, the whale was originally intended for the enjoyment of family members only. After local kids kept sneaking in for a dip, Davis hired some lifeguards, opened a small snack stand, and began charging a nominal fee for admission. Visitors loved to climb in and out of its grinning mouth and clamber through the portholes in its side. Inside, a ladder led to a loft. At the rear, a diving board allowed the daring to flip off from the tail. Families could pitch tents on the shore and picnic at concrete tables installed around the banks. Unfortunately, the park closed in 1988 when it became too much to handle. *Author*

genuine leather moccasins. For those restricted by budget, miniature cacti, saguaro preserves, and chunks of petrified wood provided shopping satisfaction. Even the children were accommodated with an assortment that rivaled the most modern toy store. Aisles stocked to the brim with tin toys, reproduction bow and arrow sets, cowboy clothes, six-shooter cap guns, wind-up drummers, feathered headbands, and articulated wood rattlesnakes were the reasons kids in the backseat begged their parents to stop!

Sometimes, the parents needed no prodding when it came to visiting the tourist traps—especially if they were the type that offered up real live Indian shows. In that department, the Cliff Dwellings Trading Post near Lookout Point, New Mexico, was one of the Route 66 favorites. There, a half-dozen authentic Indian dancers performed ceremonial routines inside a rustic stockade. Every half-hour, patrons scurried to the rear of the store to be dazzled by a boisterous demonstration of native culture. For the 1950s family trekking their way across the continent there was always ample time left in the itinerary to watch the ceremonial moves of indigenous Americans.

Unfortunately, the live Indian gala proved to be a little too disruptive for sales. While a great gimmick to pull in the crowds, it appeared that many visitors were only there to see the complimentary show. A more suitable equilibrium was attained by the trading posts when native silver-smiths, rug makers, and basket weavers were hired to perform their work on site. As visitors watched skilled artisans creating the articles sold, it instilled a marked sense of value into the handmade merchandise. It was a great method of in-store promotion, since customers could be entertained

above
In the time before the fluorescent illumination of the highway billboard cluttered the roadscape, the painted advertisement gave color to city buildings. In the urban jungle, a canvas of brick often provided the perfect spot to hawk products and services. Today, these once common examples of commercial art exist only as ghosts—unexpectedly revealed when neighboring buildings are demolished and layers of paint peel. Galena, Kansas. *Author*

left
Many small towns along Route 66 rely on the agriculture business for their revenues. On their downtown side streets, it's not at all unusual to spy feed stores and related businesses advertising their wares. Stroud, Oklahoma. *Author*

The Jackalope is more than the name of a famous Route 66 trading post. It's a mythical animal—part Jack Rabbit and part antelope —a creature that has been firmly ensconced into the western myth. According to legend, the Jackalope will sing in a human voice under a full moon. This six-foot-tall model of chicken wire and fiberglass crafted by artist Nancy Lamb sits atop a Texas business once affiliated with an outfit by the same name in Santa Fe, New Mexico. South of Route 66 near Fort Worth, Texas. *Author*

as their sales resistance was being worn down. In the end, moving souvenirs—and truckloads of them—was the primary intention of the traders doing business along Route 66.

With that goal at the forefront, there was no limit to what the roadside tourist traps would do to boost business. In the Southwestern United States—where the nervous automobile traveler feared the desert and the creatures that lived there—this fact forged an unholy alliance between the highway retailer and the reptile world. By the mid-1950s, the combination curio shop and animal farm had evolved into a hybrid business that guaranteed visitors. Its drawing card? One of the most controversial highway hypes devised by man: the snake-pit!

For farm-raised midwesterners, travelers from the East, and folks who just plain didn't get out much, nothing back home could compare to "Reptile Gardens," the ultimate trading post and slither house located in Bluewater, New Mexico. Billed as the "largest rattlesnake trading post" along the entire length of 66, it housed under one roof all the cold-blooded creatures that anyone would ever want to view during an entire lifetime!

Leading the exotic entourage, a King Cobra 15 feet long occupied the center ring, accompanied by an immense python weighing in at a whopping 200 pounds! As sideshow filler, an amazing assortment of cobras imported from India, Malaysia, and Sumatra were put on public display. Crowds marveled

America's Heyday for Hood Ornaments

"Vehicle designers combined a variety of figurals with the car radiator, crowning unadorned reservoirs of coolant with decorative 'what-nots.'"

Around 1,200 B.C., the shipbuilders of ancient Greece tipped the long, curved bows of their seagoing ships with carved figureheads. So did the Vikings of Scandinavia, crowning the keels of their oar boats with chiseled dragon heads and other creatures. It was a practice that continued well into the 19th century, when ocean vessels were routinely adorned with curvaceous mermaids and other buxom beauties.

Unfortunately, when the era of clipper ships concluded, so ended the reign of the nautical mascot. Or so everyone thought. With the advent of the motorcar, the brazen sea statues once secured to a ship's hull were reincarnated atop the hood of an automobile! Vehicle designers combined a variety of figurals with the car radiator, crowning unadorned reservoirs of coolant with decorative "what-nots." Suddenly, the exposed radiator cap became the focal point for automotive personalization!

At first, the motoring mascots were simple. Made of cheap pot metal, the earliest examples represented brand marques and logos and were introduced by a variety of car manufacturers and supply companies. Speed became the predominant theme, with winged creatures of all sorts taking perch upon the engine cowling. Projecting an aura of strength became a favorite notion as well, accomplished by affixing animal miniatures to one's vehicle. Lions, tigers, bears, and bulls were preferred. Curiously enough, any object that could be readily converted into a hood ornament became fair game, including a pair of bronzed baby shoes!

During the Art Nouveau period of the mid-1920s, French artist René Lalique fueled the mania for mascots by mating the essence of motoring's golden era with the opulent age of elegance. His first commercial entry into the genre was a piece called "Five Chevaux" (Horses), a transparent crystal decorative crafted for French automaker Citroën in 1925. Over the next decade he fashioned over two dozen designs, choosing subjects as diverse as an eagle's head and a streaking comet! But, none compared to his streamlined "Victoire," a masterful likeness of a demigod's head representing the spirit of the wind.

Realistically, only those fortunate few who could afford a Rolls or Duesenberg had the privilege of displaying a bronze or crystal mascot. For the working Joe, humorous hood ornaments were much more appropriate—and affordable! Within this category, the selection was virtually limitless. Painted reproductions of the famous Kewpie doll, whimsical traffic cops with spinning arms, figures of Donald Duck, models of Mickey Mouse, and busts of Uncle Sam were some of the exemplars. Even Britain's bug-eyed

"Dinkie Doo" was immortalized in metal plate, along with a rogue's gallery of imps (thumbing their noses) and ghoulish skulls.

When they weren't fashioned after figures, many of the novelty ornaments were gadgets of the most inventive kind. The Wiggler Company of Buffalo introduced the "spinning rotoscope," a whirly-gig featuring four, bright red, enameled, cup-shaped discs intended to twirl in the turbulent airstream. Another unusual entry from Prossi of England depicted a scaled-down lighthouse rigged so that when the brakes were applied, a tiny searchlight was illuminated. For the early off-roaders concerned about their autos' angle of incline, the "Tel-O-Grade" indicator was invaluable. Still, none were as practical as the ingenious radiator stopper constructed to house a removable pocket watch!

Despite the preponderance of these novelty radiator finials, not all mascots were intended for simple-minded amusement. Many were designed specifically to monitor the temperature of radiator water and alert the driver to an impending boil over. The Moto-Meter Company, Inc., of Long Island City, New York, manufactured some of the most widely purchased models during the 1920s and 1930s under its "Boyce Motometer" brand. Attached to the radiator, both the "Senior" and "Junior" versions featured a diminutive thermometer set within a circular housing. For the driver with good vision, a translucent cut-out (positioned over the "normal" range) allowed visual monitoring right from the comfort of one's front seat.

As the philosophy of streamlining began to redefine the shape of the motorcoach during the 1940s, the craze for hood ornaments subsided. The radiator itself was no longer an exterior design element. Now, it was hidden under a shroud of sheet metal beneath the hood. The celebrated radiator cap—once the primary point of attachment for the motoring mascot—was out of sight and out of mind. Decorative embellishments were no longer necessary.

Motorists of the late 1920s and 1930s often adorned their motorcars with whimsical hood ornaments. This devilish imp thumbs his nose at oncoming traffic, proving that even during the 1930s automobile owners pursued their own individuality when it came to accessories. Russell Lee photo, 1939. *Library of Congress*

Some of the first hood ornaments possessed a dual function quite important to the automobile owner: They gave one's flivver a distinctive look, while at the same time monitoring the water temperature in the radiator. The Moto-Meter Company of Long Island City, New York, supplied many of these devices to the consumer, its Boyce Motometer Universal Model one of the most common. Eagle's wings were, of course, optional. *Author*

Ray Meany's "Fabulous" Hopi House set the architectural standard for all other Route 66 trading posts. Constructed from adobe set in mud mortar, it was an eye-catching design that featured exposed roof timbers, an exterior staircase, and a restrained application of advertising. While most of the tourist markets along Route 66 were designed for gaining maximum attention through garish design, Meany's multilevel complex was a tasteful exception to the rule. Located 10 miles west of Winslow, Arizona, on Route 66, it was a complete tourist stop with coffee shop, motel, and Texaco-branded service station. *Preziosi Postcards*

below
Over the years, souvenir, curio, and gift shops located in the Southwestern states have borrowed extensively from the Native American heritage. In one form or another, the teepee and other Indian designs have found themselves incorporated into the visual front of many commercial structures. 924 East Tucumcari Boulevard, Tucumcari, New Mexico. *Preziosi Postcards*

at the sight of a Green Mamba, a hideous Gila monster, and dozens of fresh, squirming rattlesnakes! As a matter of course, most tourists checked their shopping bags for stowaways upon departure.

Unfortunately, the appeal of the snake shows wasn't enough to sustain the merchants when the Great Highway fell from prominence. With a growing addiction to shopping malls, franchised hamburger stands, thematic amusement parks, video games, and cruise control, the modern motorist began to view the quirky wayside attractions of yesterday's roadways as so

below
Since the days of dirt roads and wagon trains, Texas has promoted itself as being home to the biggest and the best. While there is some truth to the claim, souvenir postcards have always inflated that claim and taken it to the extreme. Stocked in curio shops along Texas 66, it wasn't at all unusual to see longhorn cattle depicted on the cards as elephantine giants, grasshoppers mutated to horse stature, and Jackrabbits big enough to ride. *Author*

much hokum. As vacationers' focus on destinations increased, interest in trading posts and other homespun attractions diminished. As the headlong rush to "get there" edged out simple enjoyment of the motor trip, the sights found along the way became a moot point.

At the same time, the concept of "entertainment" was being redefined by the flicker of images on a cathode-ray picture tube. Television had arrived with a vengeance, embracing the western myth with such vigor that within a few short years, the "home where the buffalo roam"

Trading posts along Route 66 often changed owners faster than you could fill up a water bag. Consider the establishment begun as Hopi Village: When the original owners sold out, the trading trap reopened as Howdy Hanks. Later, when Hank decided to get out of the trinket business, Sitting Bull's Indian Store became the new name. Evidence of multiple owners could be seen in the colorful advertising signs. The little men that were once astronauts were simply repainted to look like whimsical Indians! Sitting Bull quit the business, too, and the structure is now a feed store. Joseph City, Arizona, 1988. *Jerry McClanahan ©1995*

Drive-in movies used to be a big part of getting your kicks on Route 66. Out near Barstow, California, where the old road runs along the Mojave River, remnants of the past still remain for those who take the time to look. This was the section of two-lane bypassed—and effectively put out of business—when Interstate 15 was constructed between the towns of Barstow and Victorville. Route 66, Lenwood, California. *Jim Ross ©1995*

had been relieved of its mystique. Jaded by the endless shows, the sophisticated tourist was more concerned about whether the motel room off the next exit ramp came equipped with a television set rather than real hickory furniture.

As the high-speed interstates sucked the lifeblood from Route 66, the once bustling ribbon of road became nothing more than the molted skin of a bygone era. By the 1970s, the countrywide implementation (and completion) of the

continued on page 38

35

Totem Pole Park Was Nathan Galloway's Gift

"His contribution to humanity was a totem pole—a concrete-and-wire masterpiece built with an amalgam of sweat, ingenuity, and determination."

*N*athan Edward Galloway didn't discover the cure for the common cold, invent a machine to spin gold, or negotiate successfully for world peace. His contribution to humanity was a totem pole, a concrete-and-wire masterpiece built with an amalgam of sweat, ingenuity, and determination—its sole intention to make the everyday lives of people a little more enjoyable.

It was a practice that Galloway had a lot of experience with. For 22 years, he perfected his "habit of giving" as instructor of industrial arts for the Charles Page Home for Widows and Orphans in Sand Springs, Oklahoma. On a daily basis, he parceled out his precious nuggets of talent. When not guiding others, he crafted three-dimensional works for his own satisfaction, including animal sculptures, intricate pictures of wood inlay, and even violins. True to his thoughts that "the way to open doors for people is to make them something," many of these one-of-a-kind works were bestowed upon friends and acquaintances.

On days off, all of his extra time was used to develop the plot of land he owned four miles from Foyil, Oklahoma. Right alongside the unpaved cut of 28A, he continued to create—building a country home made of native stone. Six years of weekends were used laboring over the rock rambler—refining plans, fitting stones, and cutting trees. As the rustic habitat neared its completion in 1938, Galloway retired from teaching and moved with his wife to this former hobby site in rural Rogers County.

Not content to ease back in a rocking chair, his "retirement" marked the beginning of great accomplishments in the art field. Rather than continue with his usual crafts, he decided to concentrate on an idea that he had been puttering around with over the last 12 months: an immense, multistory totem pole—positioned right near the road! Motorists would be able to view it from their cars at any hour of the day, seven days a week, without charge.

It was an ambitious project to say the least. Surplus wire rescued from the railway in Sand Springs was combined with other reinforcing to form a working skeleton. In all, over six tons of steel were used to make the internal superstructure. On this bracing, Galloway hand-plastered a mortar mix that required 28 tons of cement. From a nearby creek, over 100 tons of sand and rock were hauled with a five gallon bucket!

Because specialized tools for his unique method of carving were not available, he employed some old-fashioned ingenuity to devise his own instruments from scrap metal and wood. While preliminary sculpting of the foundation's "turtle" was done with ease, carving complex reliefs near the pinnacle required more bravado. As the design stretched ever skyward, reaching the 90-foot mark with building materials proved a problem. As always, Galloway met the challenge and constructed a handy system of scaffolding and pulleys to hoist himself up!

In spite of his homemade fixtures and sometimes eccentric construction methods, the towering monolith emerged as Galloway's ultimate creation. On the exterior, 200 detailed carvings paid homage to a hodgepodge of famous Indian chiefs, mythical raptors, familiar flowers, fanciful fish, and other symbols. A bright rainbow of paint provided the finishing touch. Inside the tapered spire, murals depicting memorable events through history adorned the walls.

After eleven years, the nine-story, five-level totem pole was completed! Next, a twelve-sided edifice resembling an Indian hogan was built—providing "museum" space to house some 300 fiddles Galloway had already carved (each from a different type of wood). For lunching tourists, a whimsical road-

Edward Nathan Galloway began the construction of his giant totem pole in 1938 and finished it 11 years later. As more and more motorists took to the roads in search of recreation and adventure, it became a much-visited and admired roadside attraction and remains today as a tribute to what imagination, hard work, and purpose can achieve. Foyil, Oklahoma. *Author*

side table was crafted. To keep the totem company, a larger-than-life arrowhead (topped with weathervane) joined the menagerie of creatures in the concrete garden. Additional sculptures were planned but never built. Galloway had too many ideas left and simply not enough time to see them through.

In 1962, the artist who throughout his life petitioned others to "work on your imaginations" passed away at the age of eighty-two. On his deathbed, he summed up his attitude toward his fellow man when he wrote the words that could have well served as epitaph: "All my life I did the best I knew. I built these things by the side of the road to be a friend to you."

As a motoring Mecca for the millions of pilgrims seeking the real meaning of Highway 66, the "world's largest totem pole" has become that gift. Today, it remains an outstretched hand of friendship—put there by Edward Nathan Galloway, a folk art genius who gave himself away both in his life and in his work.

On the exterior of Ed Galloway's main totem pole, 200 detailed carvings pay homage to a hodgepodge of famous Indian chiefs, mythical raptors, familiar flowers, fanciful fish, and other symbols. A bright rainbow of paint provides the finishing touch. Inside the tapered spire, murals depicting memorable events through the walls. The totem poles are currently being restored and may still be visited. Located off of Old Route 66 on Highway 28A. Foyil, Oklahoma. *Author*

During the early 1960s, television producer Sterling Siliphant created the popular "on-the-road" program "Route 66." Featuring George Maharis and Martin Milner as two high-energy youths screaming around the countryside in an equally energetic Corvette, it epitomized the fantasy of automotive escape. From the comfort of their easy chairs, viewers across America could ride along and experience the adventures of the open road. *Personality Photos*

continued from page 35

freeways instigated by the Interstate Highway Act of 1956 brought an end to the merchandising mania of the old road. In small towns, Wal-Mart discounters usurped the obligations of the curio shops. Along the impersonal miles of the interstate, sprawling truck stops and feeding facilities assumed the responsibility of trading trinkets. Real leather products were now "crafted" in China from genuine imitation vinyl, turquoise stone became colored plastic, and the only reptiles were either flattened on the freeway or made of rubber.

A Southern Pacific railroad advertising billboard strikes an ironic contrast with a pair of migrant workers making their way along the Mother Road toward the city of Los Angeles. Down on their luck and unable to afford an automobile, many out-of-work men had no other choice but to walk during the height of the Great Depression. Dorothea Lange photo, 1937. *Library of Congress*

The Querino Canyon Trading Post is one of the ghosts of the old road decaying in Northern Arizona. Located on a stretch of road where the pavement has been removed, it's not a convenient place to stop anymore for a bottle of pop or souvenirs. The stretch of Route 66 that once ran by it has now returned to dirt. This former Chevron refueling stop was abandoned and finally burned down during the early 1990s. Querino Canyon, Arizona, 1991. *Jerry McClanahan ©1995*

Today, only a few of the tourist traps remain along the road-less-traveled. Most of the extravagant operations have long since gone out of business, their original owners retired, deceased, or disinterested. Other outfits have evolved with the times, but remain mere shadows of what they used to be. While some of the trading post structures have found new uses, the majority have been abandoned. For the adventurous motorist who steers clear of the superhighway in deference to the free road, only crumbling walls, faded murals, and fragments of neon remain as evidence of the way Americans used to get their kicks . . . on Route 66.

Miles Mahan was a retired carney and roadside character who decided to set up a little roadside "museum" along Route 66 during the 1950s. Located near Victorville, California, he called the place Hulaville and touted his big "Hula Girl" as the main attraction. Featuring an odd assortment of things he had found or visitors had left him, Mahan's unusual curiosity display was a pleasure for motorists to visit. A miniature golf course made with junk was one of the highlights, as was poet-laureate Mahan himself. Sadly, Mahan's Hulaville has become a casualty of time. Because of Mahan's advancing age and illness, the site was dismantled in 1995. Currently, the city of Victorville has most of the items packed away for safekeeping and future display. *Dan Harlow ©1995*

left

Just east of Alanreed, Texas, on the former four-lane stretch of 66 (built during the late 1940s), expansive signs once advertised all sorts of rattlesnake attractions. During the height of roadside reptile shows, the Regal Reptile Ranch was one of the most recognized. Today, the giant cobra statue that used to pull in the business holds a place of prominence in the Devil's Rope Museum of McLean, Texas. The Regal Reptile Ranch closed during the 1980s. Alanreed, Texas, 1983. *Jerry McClanahan ©1995*

During the 1950s and 1960s, the Rio Pecos Ranch Truck Terminal was one of the classic truck stops along Route 66. Out front, a gigantic neon sign featured a cartoon semi truck with an attached trailer. Up on the sign, the truck cab itself was outlined with neon tubing as were the wheels. Inside the cab sat an engaging little character that looked a lot like Howdy Doody. Santa Rosa, New Mexico, 1993. *Jerry McClanahan ©1995*

below
During the golden years of the Highway 66 trek, the Tomahawk Trading Post billed itself as "the most complete comfort stop along Highway 66." It was a claim substantiated: on the premises, a full-service filling station featured gasoline at trucker's rates and, of course, clean rest rooms. All at one stop, tourists traveling by car could eat in a restaurant, shop at a small grocery store, down beers in a cocktail lounge, and shop for curios in a well-stocked trading post. Twenty-one miles west of Gallup, New Mexico, in Lupton, it really was the first and last stop out of Arizona. *Preziosi Postcards*

Linen postcards manufactured by the Curt Teich postcard company have emerged as desirable mementos of the old road. Throughout the decades of motor travel, countless tourists purchased these colorful remembrances from curio shops, five-and-dime stores, and other roadside attractions to mail off to friends and relatives back home. With many of the original sights along the highway lost, they exist as two-dimensional time-capsules of the way things used to be along our blue highways. *Preziosi Postcards*

And Then There Were Traffic Signals

"Designed for overhead suspension on a single span of wire, the classic traffic light featured heavy-duty wiring and a cast-aluminum housing."

The world's first traffic signal flickered to life on a bustling street corner in Westminster, England, in 1868. As the story goes, horse-drawn surreys, pushcarts, pedestrians, and other vehicles were clogging the square outside the Houses of Parliament. To alleviate the crossing hazard for elected officials, signaling engineer and idea-man J.P. Knight was contracted to design and construct a device to regulate the flow.

The contraption was simple enough, appearing very much like the typical railway signal of the era. Two moveable "semaphore arms" and a small lamp compartment were mounted atop a tall pipe. A policeman was required to operate the device manually, moving the location of the alert flags by means of a mechanical linkage as well as switching the rotating, colored lenses.

During daylight, the position of the metal flags indicated whether to proceed with caution or to stop. When these flared appendages were fixed downward, persons "in charge of vehicles and horses" were to continue with care—keeping constant watch for foot passengers. Extended flags indicated the "all-stop," alerting traffic to halt and pedestrians to cross. At night, the green and red lamps took over these functions, green representing the caution and red the stop.

Members of Parliament adored the device and marveled at its seemingly flawless operation for almost a year. Then—just when it seemed the traffic problem had been licked—disaster struck. A discrepancy with the gas-illumination system caused the traffic gadget to explode, blowing both the signal device and the assigned duty officer to smithereens! After news of the tragedy spread, a lack of volunteers to operate a new signal marked the end of England's experimentation with street signals.

More than four decades later, the signal saga continued in the United States. According to one account, the first red and green traffic lights were installed in Salt Lake City by policeman Lester Wire in 1912. Even so, The American Traffic Signal Company claims that in 1914, it installed Cleveland's first electric unit (with buzzer). However, most historians give credit to inventor Garrett Morgan as Cleveland's original signal sage with his four-way creation of 1923. Regardless, the electric light replaced gas lamps in all accounts, increasing both brightness and safety.

One of America's first traffic signals appeared in the city of Detroit, Michigan, in 1914. While it was an improvement in the field of traffic control (it was really nothing more than a hand-operated "stop" light), officials still found it prudent to post a policeman with the new gadget. *Reprinted with permission of the American Automobile Mfg. Assoc.*

With the practicality of the traffic signal proven, municipalities across the nation began installing their own units. Along Fifth Avenue in New York city, gilded columns adorned with ornamental statuettes supported a trio of lights. Along the congested streets of Los Angeles, showmanship prevailed. Out there, automated traffic control went totally Hollywood and featured animated semaphore arms and clanging bells!

Despite the showy example set by America's larger cities, most towns chose to install "four-way" traffic signals. Designed for overhead suspension on a single span of wire, the classic unit featured heavy-duty wiring and a cast-aluminum housing. A quad arrangement of red, amber, and green lights (with eight-inch lenses optically engineered to inhibit reflections) allowed complete car control in all directions. From the 1930s until the 1950s, the demand from traffic departments kept manufacturers such as the Darley Company of Chicago and Eagle Signal of Moline, Illinois, busy with orders.

By the dawn of the 1960s, the increased volume of traffic on America's streets threatened the future of the four-way signal. As traffic engineers widened corridors and added turning lanes at intersections, the Federal Highway Administration revised the traffic codes. New laws called for additional signal units to be posted at all major crossings. The installation of these "dual indications" would preclude burned out bulbs or mechanical failure in a single unit.

A handful of cities circumvented the updated rules by hanging additional four-way clusters, while others dumped their "antiquated" flashers in order to collect monies offered by the Highway Trust Fund. Without concern for historic preservation or aesthetics, a majority of American municipalities went for the green and opted for the installation of updated lights. By the time motorists were stuck in long gas lines during the 1970s, most intersections were festooned with multiple constellations of lamps.

The distinctive yellow, multicolor four-way traffic light had blinked its way into obscurity, an unfortunate casualty of progress. It was now a novelty—a nostalgic relic destined for use along abandoned main streets and in towns time forgot. Quiet stretches of roadway (like old 66) became its final domain, where, swaying gently to and fro in the breeze, it continued to wink in memory of the way motoring used to be.

During the early 1910s and on into the 1920s, corduroy roads were a familiar sight for automobile owners endeavoring to cross the desert by automobile. To form a driveable surface, planks of wood were arranged in an assembled structure that sat on top of the earth. When two cars met on narrow portions of the roadbed coming in opposite directions, it was prudent to keep one set of wheels on the wood to prevent one's car from being stuck in the sand. Near Yuma, Arizona, circa 1925. *Library of Congress*

Migratory cotton pickers travel the old road to connect with Highway 99 between Tulare and Fresno, California. This driver and his family have motored the Mother Road all the way from Independence, Kansas, and have been in California for six months looking for work. When this photo was taken in 1939, the family was off to find employment chopping cotton. Merced, California, Dorothea Lange photo, 1946. *Library of Congress*

"The Route 66 Travel Game" features the smiling faces of Martin Milner and George Maharis streaking over the blacktop in a cherry Corvette convertible. Originally intended for players between the ages of 8 and 12, it was marketed by the prominent game manufacturer Transogram and was sold in toy stores when the "Route 66" television series was at the height of its popularity in the early 1960s. Inside, car-shaped game pieces and colorful play money complement a playing field that takes travelers from a garage in Los Angeles all the way to Las Vegas. In the process, towns along the length of 66 are visited, bringing monetary penalties and rewards. *Courtesy Warren Winthrop*

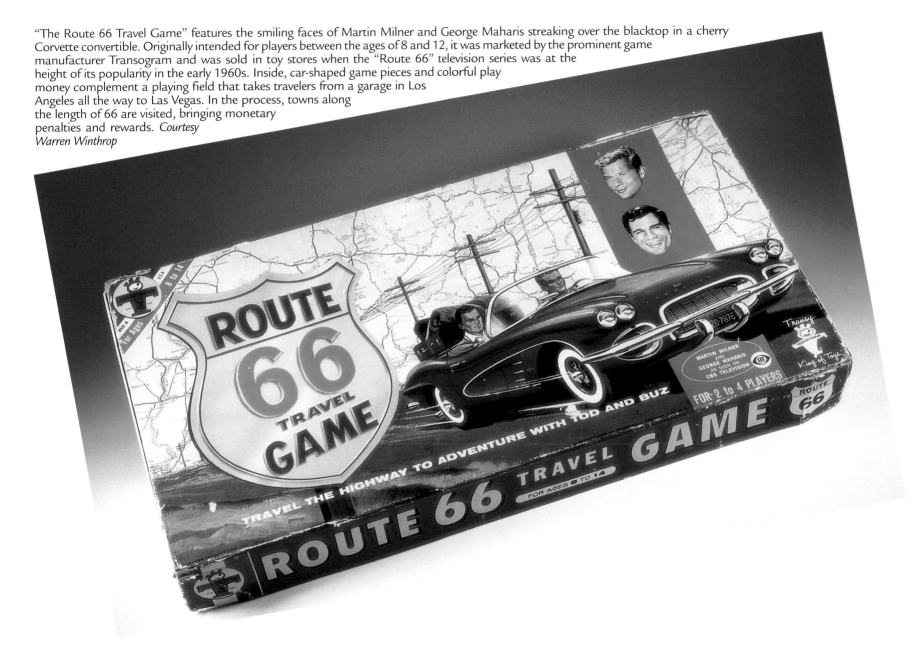

chapter two

Virtually, this is how Chicago grew: around a trading-post. May it not be that new villages and towns and, ultimately, cities will grow up around some of the best located of our roadside filling stations? It is conceivable that they will, for they are generally on highways that are served by modern bus transportation, swift and flexible. And near many of them flat fields are available for airports. A center need no longer be located on a railroad in order to develop into an important spot on the map. Watch the roadside filling stations of America . . . many of them may even now be cities in embryo."

—-The Literary Digest, "Filling Stations as Embryo Cities," 1930

Filling Stations:
Highway Pump and Circumstance

In 1904, Missouri motorists who sought adventure out along the "Old Wire Road" faced considerable adversity. That year, the U.S. Office of Road Inquiry reported that out of the 2,151,570 miles of roads nationwide, 93 percent were comprised entirely of dirt. The passage winding its way south from St. Louis to Joplin was no exception. Nothing more than a cleared course with soil at its base, it was a path frequented by horse-drawn carriage, delivery wagon, or other conveyance pulled by animal power.

A clean windshield has always been a primary concern for the motorist traveling by automobile over Highway 66. During the 1940s, service stations still had an emphasis on "service." A large part of that service was washing, drying, and buffing the window glass to a sparkling sheen. Cairo, Illinois, Arthur Rothstein photo, 1940. *Library of Congress*

left
During the early years of the horseless carriage, the country store was one of the businesses where motorists could purchase gasoline. Along with soap powder, grain, biscuits, and thread, the owners of a motorcar could stop in front of a tall, visible-register gasoline pump and have their tank refilled. Because fledgling oil companies didn't want to spend the huge amounts of capital required to obtain real-estate, existing retail operations were solicited to sell motor fuel and associated products. It was a system that worked—until competition necessitated the move to an arrangement that catered strictly to the automobile. Soon, specialized structures like this modern Phillips station of the 1950s housed power lifts, mechanics, and car accessories all under one roof. Route 66, 36th and Shartel, Oklahoma City, Oklahoma. *Courtesy Phillips Petroleum Company*

For the automotive enthusiast, driving this future alignment of Highway 66 was arduous. Jagged rocks and other road hazards wreaked havoc on fragile balloon tires. When the rains came, wheels tilled the unprotected roadbed into a treacherous bog of mud. In the frenzy to keep rolling, axles snapped, radiators bubbled over, and engines blew up. At the turn of the century, transportation corridors were ill-suited for the horseless carriage.

To make matters worse, service amenities were scarce. Carriage works had headquarters in larger cities, as did the livery stables and bicycle shops that often carried car accessories sought by the motoring crowd. Because there were no specialized car repair garages to speak of, vehicle owners were required to be mechanical experts. Fixing an automobile between towns was a frequent occurrence.

Still, the ingenuity of the motorcar operator could only go so far. A motor might very well be repaired en route if it failed—but when the fuel supply in one's gasoline tank dipped below a safe level, nothing more could be done. Since the average motor coach of the age could only travel about 70 miles on a full tank of gas, an additional canister filled with an emergency supply of fuel was always carried along. A second tin of lubricating oil was usually stored under

Vintage gasoline dispensers are becoming an extremely rare commodity along our modern roadscape. Suddenly, yesterday's machinery has become tomorrow's treasure—a fact of life dictating the hasty removal of anything and everything deemed valuable from the narrow shoulders lining this nation's asphalt. This dispenser pumped fuel (for station use only) at the Wagon Train Automotive shop near Cajon Pass, California. *Jerry McClanahan ©1995*

the seat. Once these reserves were consumed, luck—or clever timing—played a large part in completing the journey.

To enable automobile owners to experiment with their "horseless car-

riages," small quantities of gasoline were sold in pre-filled containers at drugstores, general merchandise suppliers, blacksmith shops, and other vendors in major cities like Missouri's Stanton, Waynesville, and Carthage. But unlike the modern service station markets of today, retailers that stocked motor fuel were in business mainly to sell other products—gasoline was an insignificant sideline. Motoring was still considered a pastime for those with money to burn.

In most instances, the enthusiastic car lover turned to an operation known as the "bulk depot." In a commercial setting, the major oil refiners sold a variety of processed petroleum products—including kerosene, axle grease, motor oil, and gasoline. Usually situated in the sparsely populated area of town near the railroad tracks or on the outskirts, they were more sympathetic to the awkward task of refilling an automobile's fuel tank. No one raised a concern over a gasoline-stained driving coat or boots splattered with oil. Since most of the business was conducted on an outdoor lot in the open air, appearances didn't matter.

At the bulk depot, motor spirits were stored in a large cylindrical storage vessel perched atop a wooden support structure. To refill a car's gas tank, a depot operator—who wasn't afraid to soil his trousers—drained gas into a portable can of five gallons or less provided by the car owner. Gingerly, this canister was carried to the parked vehicle. Next, one

above
In a scene straight out of *The Grapes of Wrath*, a migrant farm worker from Chickasaw, Oklahoma, is stalled in the Southern California desert with no money, no extra gasoline, and no prospect for work. He and his 10 children are facing an unknown future in the fields of California. Dorothea Lange photo, 1937. *Library of Congress*

Although the introduction of the visible register gas pump was an improvement over "blind" pumps, they were still subject to cheating. Disreputable stations doing business in tourist trap towns could readily place a brick or other object in the tank, inflating gallon readings to the operator's advantage. More sinister schemes included the misalignment of the measuring rack or improper numbering. Still, customers had certain advantages as well: During the heat of the day, warm motor fuel would register higher in the tank. As a result, it was advantageous to fill up in the cool of the morning and get the most volume for one's money. *Courtesy Tokheim Corporation*

The Rest Haven Motor Court is a typical example of the tourist court and gas station combination so prevalent during the 1940s and 1950s. No doubt, the gleaming box-style Phillips station was the first structure built, followed by rows of overnight cabins. With five gasoline pumps and an interior gift shop taking the place of the usual auto accessories, it was obviously an outfit designed for maximum revenue and product turnover. Springfield, Missouri. *Preziosi Postcards*

The Hi-Line Modern Motor Court was located where U.S. 66 meets U.S. 89 in Ashfork, Arizona. This advertising postcard touted "New, strictly modern cottages with and without equipped kitchenettes." Of course, tiled showers and closed, attached garages made staying overnight a joy. Twin Wayne 60 gasoline pumps and a matching Art-Deco sign pulled in customers low on gasoline. *Courtesy Chuck Sturm*

assistant steadied a large funnel on the filler tube and helped to guide the liquid into the tank. To trap sediment and other debris, a second helper thrust a piece of chamois or other makeshift filter over the funnel. A third person tipped the storage can and with great care, began pouring the precious gasoline into the automobile.

Because there was no accurate method devised to alert the pourer as to when he should stop, fuel spilled over hands and clothing and often onto the automobile itself. Wooden measuring sticks marked with indications gauged to a handful of popular tank sizes helped, while at the same time creating more peripheral equipment prone to accidental ignition. Patrons

Pay Less for Gas at Hedges

GAS 25½ 28½ 30½

HEDGES OIL CO.

WE HONOR ALL OIL COMPANY CREDIT CARDS

REG 28½   GAS 25½

The Hedges Oil Company chain of gas stations had a small network of 16 gasoline stations in major New Mexico cities. With heavily discounted prices and clean rest room lounges for the ladies, they did a thriving business during the postwar surge of vacations taken by automobile owners. Albuquerque, New Mexico. *Preziosi Postcards*

careless with an open flame caused horrific fires, greatly limiting the appeal of motoring to a brave minority.

Thankfully, progress was being made to replace this crude refueling method of "drum and measure." The changes began almost one year after the Office of Road Inquiry's report when entrepreneurs Clem Laessig and Harry Grenner debuted a radically new type of fuel depot in 1905. They called their operation the Automobile

Gasoline Company and began recruiting customers motoring in and out of the bustling trading hub of St. Louis.

Their location would prove to be a good one: the meandering telegraph route that was to be designated as part of the Ozark Trails (and later Highway 66) was nearby. It was a perfect location to get the attention of the growing legions of car owners taking to the roads. As the popular bromide of the time boasted:

The American roadways have always been rich with signs and billboards attempting to capture the motorist's attention. When these painted message boards fail to shock or amuse, one of the last methods they employ is an appeal to the pocketbook—a direct hit for many travelers motoring long-distances on a budget. Attention-grabbing slogans such as "Never Undersold" or "Our Prices Can't Be Beat" play on the price-conscious driver, already low on cash from the gouging experienced at the overpriced greasy spoons and motels along the route. For the harried traveler, it's often hard to compare prices when far from home. When the fuel gauge drops below the empty mark and the kids in the backseat are crying for a rest room, the world of choices found along the road shrinks to what's accessible within the next two miles. Santa Fe, Dorothea Lange photo, 1938. *Library of Congress*

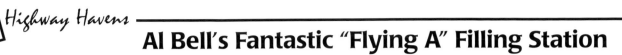
Al Bell's Fantastic "Flying A" Filling Station

"Beneath the glow, the promised land of petroleum awaited new arrivals—complete with four service islands, twelve fuel pumps, and five drive-through lanes."

For travelers cruising into Kingman on a hot summer's eve, Al Bell's "Flying A" Service Station appeared to be a roadside apparition—one that belonged more on the Las Vegas strip than the quiet community of Hilltop, Arizona. The reason? A double-sided, 209-bulb, show-stopping sign featuring a swooping arrow lit with sequential flashers. Below, blazing tubes of neon announced the promise of refreshment to desert drivers. "Jugs Iced Free" really hooked them in!

From Memorial Day until the last week of September, the elevated sparkler illuminated the Arizona nights. Luckily, Bell worked out a deal with his oil supplier to cover the cost of the staggering electric bill. It proved a beneficial arrangement, since the three story signpost pulled over $150 worth of raw current in just one month! A more power-hungry (or memorable) marquee could not be found along the entire expanse of the Will Rogers Highway.

During the dog days of summer, hundreds of vehicles in need of service were drawn by the sight—many coasting in on fumes and a prayer. Beneath the glow, the promised land of petroleum awaited new arrivals—complete with four service islands, twelve fuel pumps, and five drive-through lanes. Four attendants decked out with bow ties and white overalls (names embroidered on the breast pocket) serviced the cars simultaneously. While the first pump jockey inquired whether he could "fill it with 100-plus octane," a second lad proceeded to wipe the windows crystal clear. Meanwhile, a third checked the tire pressure as the fourth topped off the crankcase.

As the ultimate in American gas station service was being perfected, Bell's young son Bob sprinted out to the driver's side window and poked in his head. "Got any jugs you want iced?" A heavy-duty York ice machine cranked out the precious cubes at the steady rate of 450 pounds per day—providing a summer job for the enthusiastic Little Leaguer. In exchange for tips, he began toting the frozen crystals to the cars when he was only nine years old and worked every season until high school graduation.

Bob Boze Bell recalls those days with fondness: "What was amazing about working at the station was that everybody during the 1950s was bound for California. Many thought it was the promised land out there. You could see it in their eyes. During July, it was around 103 degrees in Kingman and they would all get out of their cars wilted from the heat and ask, 'How far to California?' I'd say, 'About 60 miles.' Almost every time, they would smile and blurt out, 'Oh . . . thank God!' Well, I didn't have the heart to tell them that 60 miles away was California all right—the inferno town known as Needles, California, one of the hottest locations on the planet other than Death Valley!"

But everybody asked those questions. What really stood out about the Flying A station was the sheer adventure of just working there. One afternoon, Bob was filling up a tank when he heard sirens. With filler nozzle in hand, he

The year was 1947 when Al Bell got hooked up with a Whiting Brothers station down in McConnico along the old road. It pumped out a fair amount of gallonage, but not enough for Bell. At the end of nine months, he mastered the refueling basics and decided to move on to a more lucrative position. A Mobil station on the Walapai Indian Reservation in Peach Springs, Arizona, became his new responsibility, this time in a leasing arrangement. A couple of tourist cabins out back provided extra income, and later—trouble. Young Bob Bell was playing where he wasn't supposed to and got his hand caught in the maid's washing machine wringer! They rushed him to the nearest doctor in Kingman and fortunately, his arm was saved. *Courtesy Allen P. Bell*

observed Floyd Cisney (local highway patrolman, Little League coach, and part-time driver in the demolition derby) pull up alongside a speeding car, pass it, and turn—forcing both vehicles off the road. "That part of 66 was a bottleneck for hot cars," remembers Bell. "Cisney held the record for nabbing stolen vehicles with over 5,000 arrests to his credit!"

For Bob's dad, the station was a rewarding adventure of another kind. In 1959, he attained his goal of bringing in $100 a day. When Tidewater Oil analyzed his receipts, they bluntly told him that he was "makin' too much money!" When their demands for new lease terms elevated into a fight, Bell walked—taking his service station savvy along with him. Another operator took control of the circuit breakers and as Bob Bell so aptly describes, "the Flying A went successfully downhill." Al Bell proved that there was much more to running a gas station than simply flicking on a flashy sign.

Eventually, Phillips Petroleum purchased the Associated Flying A stations in the West and the winged trademark glided into obscurity. But that wasn't important. The 1960s were half over, the country was undergoing radical changes, and Al Bell was retiring from the business of refueling. He was having problems with his legs and his doctor advised him to hit the bleachers.

Still, it didn't really matter that the highway was losing one of its heroes. When the implementation of freeways rerouted traffic around Kingman, the classic pumping venues were already relieved of their status as highway havens. After the great river of cars flowing along 66 reduced to a trickle, there weren't enough customers to keep the refuelers profitable. By then, classic gasoline oases typified by Al Bell's fantastic Flying A filling station were relegated to memories. The age of self-service had begun.

Working for tips, Al Bell's son, Bob, spent most of his childhood toting ice at the Flying A. Curiously enough, the pocket change paled in comparison to the goodies picked up by other means: Every other day, another customer would ask if they could trade gas for merchandise. "We're out of money and we gotta' make it to California," they all said. Bob's dad was sympathetic to their plight and always found something he could use in exchange for a tankful. The great highway brought in more stuff than could ever be imagined, including a set of WWII binoculars, cameras, a Bowie knife, drums, fishing poles . . . everything boys dream of. Kingman, Arizona. *Courtesy Allen P. Bell*

Clines Corners on Highway 66, New Mexico

"The world passes through St. Louis!" While much of that traffic was powered by beasts of burden, it would soon be dominated by the internal combustion engine. Gasoline—and large quantities of it—would be required to feed the coming onslaught of automobiles.

With experience in the business as bulk fuel distributors, Laessig and Grenner witnessed for themselves the growing demand for the "waste product" gasoline. As more and more piston-powered carriages appeared streetside, they acknowledged the limitless potential of the motorcar and endeavored to change the onerous refueling procedure.

Clines Corners is one of the oldest establishments along Highway 66. During the 1940s, it was equipped for "super service to the motoring public" and included one of the most modern cafes and curio shops. Roy Cline founded the New Mexico tourist stop back in the late 1920s. Today, it still exists as a souvenir shop and refueling oasis along 66 and features nothing more than a couple of gas stations and a sprawling gift shop. The "town" of Clines Corners is merely a place for those traveling by motorcar to stop and spend. Clines Corners, New Mexico. *Courtesy Chuck Sturm*

To achieve this goal, they devised a process that took the art of refueling to the next level: First, an upright storage vessel about the size of a small hot water heater was used to store the gasoline—fed from a larger tank nearby. This upright container was fitted with a hand-operated valve at its base, connected to what looked very much like an ordinary "garden" hose. When a car drove in to be refueled, an employee placed the end of this hose into the customer's gas tank. Then, he opened the spigot and let gravity push fuel directly into the stomach of the famished flivver.

Up and down the pathway of old 66, the service station attendant appeared in a variety of forms. Many donned the one-piece overall and cloth cap, while others were adorned in fancy uniforms and elaborate hats. Fifty years ago, they all had one thing in common: Take care of the customers and make sure they return. Along old 66 in Oklahoma. *Author*

At long last, motorists could steer into a roadside business and have their tanks refilled without the bother associated with visiting the bulk depot. Because cars could pull up right next to the small holding tank, metal cans once used to pour fuel remained strapped to the sideboard. The cumbersome funnel was history, along with the chamois screen that "filtered" out contaminants. Now, an integral filter system ensured that the gasoline served was pure. Missouri—and the highway that would rise to glory as America's Main Street—finally had its first real "filling station."

By the time Route 66 was officially commissioned in 1926, the filling station had evolved into a self-contained business format *continued on page 60*

Imagine pulling into a gasoline station and having your car serviced by multiple attendants! For today's jaded motorist, it's the stuff of which dreams are made. However, during the 1950s, it was no dream: Phillips stations like this classic full-server in the company territories along Route 66 sold products with an unparalleled style and grace. Wiping the windows, checking the oil, airing up the tires, and topping off the fluid in the radiator was all part of the deal. Will Rogers Airport, Oklahoma City. *Courtesy Phillips Petroleum Company*

Chronicle of the American Roadmap

"By the time the roadmap entered its heyday in the 1930s, virtually every refueling stop along Route 66 offered colorful gatefolds to its patrons."

*E*mperor Augustus of Rome knew a great road map when he saw one. Mounted on his private bedroom wall was what most historians agree constituted the most elaborate highway diagram ever created. Artfully engraved upon a sheet of hammered gold, glistening lines described the empire's entire network of transport. Principle towns were highlighted with rubies. Secondary settlements were marked with emeralds.

Though not as ostentatious, the simple road map manufactured of ink and paper was just as precious to the intrepid motorist attempting to navigate America's early trails. No self-respecting automobilist would leave civilization without one, unless he knew exactly where he was going and what facilities he could count on for gas, food, and lodging. During the early teens, crude roads or "blazed trails" were the only paths overland. Routes were poorly marked—if at all. Becoming lost out on the fringes was the rule.

Progress was made, however, when pioneering motorists with similar interests banded together. With an eye toward improving roadways and the maps that defined them, organizations such as the Automobile Association of America introduced road guides in an effort to assist members. In 1910, AAA debuted its "Official Automobile Blue Book" featuring multiple maps. These state and regional charts were well received by horseless carriage enthusiasts, despite the often arcane instructions used to guide adventurers.

With the lack of any real system to classify and designate corridors of travel, well-traveled routes were routinely navigated by means of "landmarks." Guidebooks described directions in relation to natural formations such as cliffs, boulders, and streams. These geographical features provided reliable reference points, along with man-made structures of substantial design such as buildings, bridges, or windmills.

Still, it was tough going for the motorist. Typical guide entries could alternate between clear or cryptic depending on the reference features. A typical entry might have read: "drive 6-1/2 miles, turn right at the school house, proceed 10 miles, then turn left at the stone wall." When visual aids such as directional arrows and photographs were added, the guides improved—marginally. Swelling to more than 1,000 pages with the extraneous information, impracticality soon outweighed any usefulness.

Around the same time, automobile manufacturers, tire companies, and even some motels, began passing out complimentary maps to regular customers. While less detailed than the complicated guidebooks, they were nonetheless welcomed by the motorist. After all, they were free! It didn't take long for the promotional frenzy to command the attention of petroleum refiners: In 1914, Gulf Oil joined corporate trendsetters such as White Motor and Pierce-Arrow in the practice of distributing gratuitous road diagrams.

It all started when Pittsburgh advertising guru William B. Akin advised Gulf Oil to distribute free maps to prospective customers. Executives liked the idea, and as fast as they could print a double-sided, tri-fold mailer it was delivered to 10,000 registered motorists residing in Pennsylvania's Allegheny County. Business at Gulf's drive-in service station (it was its first) boomed!

With Akin's idea proven, additional roadmaps were quickly drawn up for Pennsylvania, New York, New Jersey, and New England. A total of 300,000 were handed out to customers by Gulf's friendly service station attendants or delivered by mail.

By the time the roadmap entered its heyday in the 1930s, virtually every refueling stop along Route 66 offered colorful gatefolds to its patrons. Romanticized renderings of classic pumpers graced the covers along with exaggerated visions of powerful motorcars cresting hills and swooping through racy curves. Motorists inebriated with the thrill of driving (and purchasing gas) were depicted in their convertibles—smiling, waving, scarves flying—enjoying life to the fullest. The image of the square-jawed pump jockey was quickly becoming an American icon.

Regrettably, the colorful heyday was doomed to extinction. The famed oil embargo of the 1970s dealt the first blow with long gas lines delivering the knock-out punch. For the oil conglomerates, free maps had suddenly become an unnecessary expense, liability, even an embarrassment. Policies embracing the promotion of motoring and the massive consumption of motor fuel were suddenly no longer commercially viable. Refined gasoline was to be conserved, saved, and revered. The cartographic canvas of the free, service station roadmap was an advertising medium that had outlived its usefulness.

Automobile aficionados who found themselves traveling just south of the La Bajada Lava Cliffs during the year 1911 did not have the luxury of reaching into the glove compartment and pulling out a service station road map. During the 1910s, guidebooks detailing motoring roads were rare and many routes in remote areas were as yet, undocumented. Back then, a good sense of direction and a compass were two of the best things a vehicle owner could possess. New Mexico, A.L. Westgard photo. *National Archives*

"HIGHEST TEST"
*at the price of
ordinary gasoline*

FRANKLY, our biggest job is to get motorists to buy their first trial tankful of Phillips 66...the GREATER GASOLINE. After that, our task is simple—they always come back for more.

They prove for themselves that this gasoline is an amazing performer. That it delivers more mileage, smoother running, and extra power. They learn how Phillips CONTROLLED VOLATILITY gives higher test, from 60.6° to 71.4°. Without higher cost. So you save money by stopping at the Orange and Black 66 shield.

Phillips Highway of
MISSOURI
1933

Compliments of
Phillips Petroleum Company

PHILLIPS 66 ETHYL
*- the new HIGHEST TEST-
at the regular price
of Ethyl gasoline*

TODAY in one gasoline you can get all the famous Phillips 66 advantages —year 'round easy starting, quick acceleration, power and mileage— plus "no-knock" performance. The quality of an Ethyl gasoline depends upon the qualities of the original gasoline to which it is added. Phillips 66 Ethyl is the only Ethyl that gives you Phillips 66 performance. Makes new cars perform as the manufacturer intended and gives new pleasure in driving an old motor.

Power, no-knock, extra miles—all in Phillips 66 Ethyl. Dispensed from sealed tanks to protect you against substitution.

When the roadside service station in America was in the midst of its teenage years, road maps were colorful tools intended to aid motorists with their driving pleasure. Every imaginable theme was used for artwork, including young women in beachwear. Of course, the designs never strayed from one of the most important parts of the journey: the ever-present automobile was always pictured somewhere in the foreground. **1933 Missouri Road Map.** *Courtesy Phillips Petroleum Company*

Back in the "good old days," tourists traveling the old road for pleasure relied on the service station road map to find their way. Today, the maps remain as unique artifacts of **Route 66.** *Author*

The life of Two Guns, Arizona, was directly linked with Route 66 and the amount of traffic that passed. During the zenith of highway touring in America, it was a must-see tourist attraction for vacationers, traveling salesmen, and truck drivers speeding across the country. Caged lions, bobcats, and other wild desert animals were the settlement's main drawing cards, backed up by the obligatory restaurant and filling station. After the freeways decimated the flow of cars along old 66, business dropped and eventually ended. Another highway tourist trap bit the dust. Two Guns, Arizona. *Shellee Graham ©1995*

Two Guns got its name from a man named Two-Gun Miller who claimed to be an Apache Indian. During an argument with a neighbor, he killed the man and was later acquitted of all charges. On the grave marker, friends of the dead man wrote "Killed by Indian Miller." Miller found out, got mad, and decided to put his own epitaph on the marker. Much to his chagrin, he was subsequently thrown in jail for defacing a grave. Folklore has it that he lived for years in a cave along the banks of the Canyon Diablo. Two Guns, Arizona. *Courtesy Paul Taylor*

continued from page 56

along the road. In the interim, the gasoline dispenser had progressed far from its humble beginnings. Now with a chassis made of forged steel, brass fittings, and a silhouette of

curves, it exuded a living presence! All along America's highways, the era of the "visible register" gasoline pump was beginning.

Originating from the "blind pumps" developed by inventors in the early part of the century, the visible register gasoline pump addressed many of the motorist's concerns: Customers wanted to see the gasoline that was pouring into their tank—and rightly so. For years, unscrupulous operators were rigging indicator dials to give false gallon readings and watering down motor fuel with other liquids.

With the visible register, consumer confidence blossomed. Perched high atop a

By 1940, over 500 of Texaco's stations were built or revamped to architect Walter Dorwin Teague's specifications. With the precision of a machine, the gleaming white streamlined box was soon to become the exalted form of gas station architecture. The house as dominant identity for the American refueling business had seen the end of its days. With all cosmetic disguises lifted, the roadside building with gas pumps out front now appeared to be exactly what it was: a place to buy gasoline. No longer was it a Grecian monument, a Chinese Pagoda, or a country cottage. Erick, Oklahoma, 1983. *Jerry McClanahan ©1995*

heavy base formed of cast iron, a cylindrical crucible of glass served as a transparent holding tank for gasoline. Within this elevated bowl, graduated markings "registered" (in gallon intervals) the amount of distilled liquid pumped from an underground storage tank. Motorists could actually see the product, inspect its quality, and measure its volume with their own eyes!

When the desired amount for sale was reached, the pump operator turned a lever to release the fuel. Through a flexible rubber hose, the precious fluid gurgled into the car's gas tank. For the few who remember what it was like, there was nothing like

seeing your gasoline before it was pumped into your motorcar!

With the physical and technical aspects of refueling an automobile streamlined, it was easy for anyone to get into the sales business. Free from excessive regulations

George Morrow made his move in 1932 at the height of the Depression. Money earned from a trucking operation was rolled over into what was to become an automobile service station. The plot of land chosen was a prime piece of Route 66 real estate obtained at the price of $1,500, a site right on the West Kearney "Bypass." Since money and materials were tight, he decided to take the advice of agricultural extension booklets and build his station of unshaped fieldstone and fossilized "worm rock." West of Springfield, Missouri. *Courtesy Joe Morrow*

These days, classic station scenes from our roadside past are becoming more and more infrequent. Vintage Pepsi-Cola and Dr. Pepper signs like these are now treasured collectibles—along with the visible register unit still intact within this frame. Taken by photographer Harold Corsini in 1946 for Standard Oil of New Jersey, this Mannford, Oklahoma, refueling stop has seen its share of customers bound for glory on the Mother Road. *Courtesy Standard Oil (New Jersey) Co. Collection, Photographic Archives, University of Louisville.*

and licensing procedures, a prospective gasoline seller could make a deal with an oil refiner on Monday, have a trio of gasoline pumps delivered on Wednesday, and begin selling gas on Friday. As a result, proprietors made deals with multiple refiners. At certain points along Route 66, so-called "gasoline alleys" appeared overnight—distinguished by rows of gas pumps each dis-

playing a different brand of fuel. Route 66 was suddenly awash with gasoline.

Despite the mad rush to secure marketing arrangements, many gas stations decided to channel their energies into other directions. Rather than concentrate solely on the sale of gasoline (and hand over the bulk of revenues to the oil refiners), family operations found it profitable to offer food to the motorist. With customers frequently inquiring as to where one could get a good meal, many station owners began making sandwiches in back room kitchens and stocking soda pop.

Point-of-purchase items such as cigarettes and candy were added and before too long, the business that began as a filling station had evolved into a full-service cafe. By the time an expanded dining room, full-time cook, waitress, and jukebox were added to the equation, the trio of gasoline pumps that stood beneath the neon "Eats" sign were forgotten.

Some gasoline stops took notice of the lack of private roadside accommodations and decided to get into the business of lodging. Proprietors realized that there was much more to serving the vehicle owner than just offering a full tank of gasoline, quart of oil, or new fan belt. A good night's rest was an important part of completing the journey.

During the 1940s, when roadside services were not yet perfected, finding a rest room along the highway was difficult. Tourist camps were some of the first to erect public toilets for their customers—a precursor to the era when gasoline service stations would take care of the motorist's personal needs. Near the Old Road, Missouri, John Vachon photo, 1942. *Library of Congress*

The Fastest Filling Station in the West

*"Capable of handling virtually any service station assignment, the rolling refueler
turned every parking space into a potential garage."*

By the mid-1960s, the majority of refueling stops hustling gas along Route 66 shared a common denominator: They were "stations," that is fixed businesses at unchanging roadside positions. In order to get service, vehicles had to leave the road, drive across an air hose, and park near a fuel dispenser. No accommodations were made for the occasional automobile stranded miles down the road.

Enter inventor and service station proprietor Raymond Dietz of Borger, Texas. It was his position that if the customers couldn't make the trip to him, he would drive his entire station out to them! The key to this radical new strategy was a late-model, open-bed Ford Econoline van. Fitted with the latest equipment required to refuel, repair, and maintain a modern motorcar, the "Service Station on Wheels" rumbled out on its maiden voyage in early 1964. Selling gas would never be the same.

At first, the motorists moving south on state Highway 117 (on their way to Route 66) didn't know what to think of it. While the curious rescue rig appeared to be a truck, it featured an arrangement never before seen. On both body side-panels, a bold Phillips 66 insignia lent the vehicle an official air. At the same time, dual racing stripes of white and orange hinted at speed. Overhead, a small triangular canopy copied the architectural stylings of the refiner's turnpike superstations. Filling station apparatus—and plenty of it—filled the small rectangular bed space behind the driver's seat.

Bolted onto the truck bed, a full-sized gasoline pump of the Bowser brand poked up as its most prominent feature. Identical to the units installed at stationary applications, it sported a flexible hose, electric motor, and digital calculator. For extended roadside sales, two specialized storage containers held a considerable supply of gasoline. The main tank contained 110 gallons of Phillips 66 and a smaller receptacle the premium Flite-Fuel. To allow an operator to switch quickly between the different grades, a selection valve was installed.

Besides convenience, operating safety was a prime consideration of the patented gas station truck. To inhibit accidental ignition of fuel reserves, the power feed for the pump motor was located away from vapors inside the truck cab. Likewise, the external electrical terminals used for boosting batteries were controlled by a starter-relay switch designed to retard sparks.

For occasional engine or suspension work, a conglomeration of tools and other fixtures were kept on board. As a result, most malfunctions encountered along the road were easily remedied—including broken fan belts, burned-out alternators, and fouled spark plugs. For structural damage, an acetylene welding torch proved invaluable. Removing tires for the repair of punctures was assisted by a Coats Iron Tireman (attached securely to the rear tailgate). A miniature air compressor with an upright tank ensured refilling to the proper pressure.

Capable of handling virtually any service station assignment, the rolling refueler turned every parking space into a potential garage. At the same time, it became a showcase for the latest automotive products: Specialized racks fastened to port and starboard held more than 40 cans of motor oil in the one-quart size. From its well-stocked "parts department," streetside patrons could select from an eclectic mix of paraphernalia, including household cleaning fluids, furniture wax, tow chains, inner tubes, windshield wiper blades, light bulbs, and even antifreeze.

Despite this marketing bonanza, the wheeled wonder remained true to its primary directive. In the process, a priceless amount of good will and free publicity spelled the promise of new customers. It didn't take a rocket scientist to figure out that if a stranded traveler were rescued on just one occasion,

About 20 years ago, oil cans were regarded as throwaway items. Those that did survive the final cut either ended up on the workbench holding screws or as a handy canister to clean dirty paint-brushes. As time progressed, a few forward-thinking individuals realized that many of these tin containers featured pleasing graphics and corporate designs. Ever so slowly, a few eccentrics saved all the cans they could get their hands on and were soon scouring garbage dumps and other locations for new ones. As they worked their new "hobby" in secret, the interest in filling stations increased. Suddenly, collecting oil cans was no longer a fringe activity. Desirability grew as values increased. For anyone interested in American road culture, the collection of oil containers became serious business. The Red Horse Museum, Kansas. *Author*

the word of mouth spread along the motorway could be a boon for business. On the return leg of the trip through town these saved customers could show their appreciation by patronizing the main Dietz & Sons Phillips 66 service station—the one permanently anchored to the roadside at 1000 South Main Street in Borger, Texas.

As traffic trickled south on the great web of feeder roads to join with the mother motorway of the mid-1960s, countless car customers were introduced to the real meaning of gasoline service. After all, Raymond Dietz was out there—somewhere—cruising the backroads and byways in search of an empty fuel tank. With one hand laid firmly on the steering wheel and another gripped tight around a pump nozzle, he and his amazing Service Station on Wheels raced to legendary status—the fastest filling station in the West!

During the mid-1950s, Raymond Dietz operated the Service Station on Wheels and literally brought the filling station to the customer. For motorists stranded along Route 66, it was a practice that brought new meaning to the term "full service"! Borger, Texas. *Courtesy Phillips Petroleum Company*

Often using whatever materials they could find (such as native worm rock, scrap lumber, or logs), jack-of-all-trade types nailed together one or two tiny cabins out behind their station house. In short order, the duties of the gas station operator expanded well beyond the task of pump jockey to part-time bellboy. With gas tanks topped off, crankcase filled with oil, and tires inflated, tired travelers rented rooms for the night. As business from tourists increased, many of these moonlighters

developed into full-fledged motor courts—relegating the sale of refined gasoline to secondary importance.

By 1931, it was clear how much gasoline had affected the development of highway commerce: In the United States, government statistics revealed that there were a total of 110,000 roadside-stand owners in operation. Out of this number, almost all were expanded from filling stations. Gasoline was transforming the face of the American road. To some, it seemed like the

The Iceberg Cafe and Gas Station was built during the mid-1930s in Albuquerque, New Mexico, on the site currently occupied by the old Lobo Movie Theater. Just east of the University of New Mexico on East Central Avenue, it was a popular hangout for college students fond of ice cream. In the late 1930s, it was moved farther up Central to the 5300 block to make way for a new development. In 1953, it was moved again to a spot just north of Albuquerque on old Highway 85, somewhere near Bernalillo. After its final relocation, the former Route 66 landmark sat neglected for many years and was finally demolished in 1972. Albuquerque, New Mexico, Russell Lee photo, 1940. *Library of Congress*

When the "gas crisis" of the 1970s ended, many of the roadside gasoline businesses that once flourished had to close their doors permanently. Now—more than 20 years later—many of these bankrupt operations can still be found along the roadways, mere shells of their former selves. Like the ruins from a lost civilization, only crumbling brick, stone, and faded paint remain to remind us of just how quickly highway commerce can change. Moriarty, New Mexico, 1983. *Jerry McClanahan ©1995*

right
For the family off to see America on the open road, saving money on gasoline was one way to make the trip last longer. Stations such as this classic three pumper (a former motel office) were once numerous along the original alignment of the Mother Road, enticing business with nothing more than honest-to-goodness low prices. How did they do it? Volume, volume, volume! Santa Rosa, New Mexico, 1983. *Jerry McClanahan ©1995*

Midas touch of motor fuel held no boundaries for the enterprising operator.

It was a false assumption. The dominance of the individually owned, diversified gas station was destined to end. Large petroleum refiners—aided by the income derived from the outlets flooding Route 66 with gasoline—were accumulating the capital needed to buy more of their own land and build additional company-owned stations. By gaining control over the majority of their outlets, marketing strategies could be standardized on a national level.

This idea was nothing new. As early as 1914, Standard Oil of California had opened a chain of 34 stations on the West Coast. In the process, they learned that factors such as station appearance, architecture,

Standard Oil of California began its gas station operations on the West Coast in 1907. Following the lead of the Automobile Gasoline Company in St. Louis, they spread up and down the coast with small, similar-looking station huts. While basic in their design and layout, Standard Oil was the first company to make the move toward the unification of station architecture throughout a wide territory. *Courtesy Chevron Corporation*

and extra amenities related directly to brand loyalty. By combining full service with knowledgeable attendants, a refueling stop could pull in more patronage and influence its existing clientele to come back. For the small-time operator with nothing more than a shack as an office and two aging gravity pumps, standardization meant the

beginning of the end.

However, the improvements implemented by the major oil refiners were not limited to attitude and aesthetics. Public rest rooms that could be used on demand became a major sales tool for the post-Depression service station. While the concrete privies erected nationwide by the Works

Progress Administration were an improvement over the home-made outhouse, they were hardly the class of bathroom refined tourists desired. Frightened by the scourge of crippling microbes, society was growing increasingly aware of the unseen germ.

In 1938, the Texaco Company addressed those fears when they debuted the "registered rest room" to the motorist. As part of a nationwide promotional blitz, each of the company's gas station bathrooms were officially registered and individually numbered. Touting the toilets as a "Texaco Dealer Service," curb placards were placed along the shoulder to attract the interest of passing vehicles. For stations in the Texaco sales territories along Highway 66, it was a sales-boosting move.

Behind doors posted with green and white rest room signs signifying "Men" and "Ladies," there existed public powder rooms without peer. Inside the sanitary compartments, tiled interiors sparkled with an unprecedented cleanliness. Modern commodes of porcelain accompanied gleaming sinks. Fully equipped with fresh soap and fluffy

When toll roads such as the Turner Turnpike took over many of Route 66's duties, a new type of highway rest stop emerged. Phillips Petroleum introduced its Vendorama stations in the early 1960s to meet the expected demand. Like the world-famous Horn and Hardart automat in New York City, the Vendoramas allowed visitors to select products from machines and serve themselves. Oklahoma City, Oklahoma. *Courtesy Phillips Petroleum Company*

When Highway 66 was in its glory, the service station attendant was a dedicated roadside servant. With a courteous smile and a friendly attitude, America's pump jockeys were expected to carry out the basic rituals required to ensure the utmost in motoring pleasure. Checking the oil level and tire pressure was required, as was checking mechanical components for signs of failure. Ensuring that the windshield was free from grease, grime, and insects was high on the list of station priorities, too. When a car pulled up to the pumps during the 1930s and 1940s, an attendant was always there to greet it. Without hesitation, the eager-to-please serviceman pleasantly inquired as to the amount of gasoline desired and set upon the task of operating the dispenser. *Courtesy Chevron Corporation*

Rock-Wool Insulated against Heat and Cold

WINTER AIR CONDITIONED CENTRAL HEAT

ON U. S. 66 and 60 at EAST CITY LIMITS, AMARILLO, TEXAS
— Authorized Standard Oil Lubrication —

J. Wilkie Talbert was the owner and manager of the Pueblo Court. Featuring ultramodern accommodations with the charm of "early American Pueblo Indian architecture and furniture," it doubled as an authorized center for Standard Oil Lubrication. An adjoining restaurant served food approved by none other than Duncan Hines himself. Amarillo, Texas. *Preziosi Postcards*

towels, the Texaco registered units delivered a new level of personal comfort.

To make sure that the pristine washrooms lived up to the ads, Texaco maintained a fleet of "White Patrol" Chevrolets. All 48 states fell under the white-glove scrutiny of these water closet watchers. Undaunted by rain, sleet, and snow— they rode the highways and byways of America so that the gas station customer would remain safe in the assurance that

their appointed rest room was free from dirt or germ.

As our nation prepared to enter World War II, Phillips Petroleum introduced its own campaign for polishing up the public privy. Its team of registered nurses ensured that all "Certified" facilities throughout the Phillips sales region were immaculate. Six of these "Highway Hostesses" took to the Will Rogers route to validate conditions at random. If they

The Fact and Fable of Phillips Motor Fuel

"An excess of amusing yarns and unbelievable anecdotes have persisted as explanations for the double-digit, road-related, brand-name choice."

*A*mong the endless catalogue of gasoline trademarks once spotted along America's Main Street, no refined motor fuel has been obfuscated with as much controversy as the Phillips gasoline brand. Ever since its first gallon of go-juice gurgled up through a visible-register fuel pump, an excess of amusing yarns and unbelievable anecdotes have persisted as explanations for the double-digit, road-related, brand-name choice.

The most common tale explaining the choice of the "66" designation is based solely on a numerical myth. This fable relates details of the first Phillips station built in Wichita, Kansas. According to the legend, the flagship refueling depot sold exactly 6,600 gallons of gas by the end of the first day's business. Supposedly, the station manager turned to a company representative standing nearby and dubbed the new fuel with the comment: "Boy, 66 is our lucky number!" Unfortunately, the report is historically inaccurate. That heartland haven for cars dispensed over 12,000 gallons on grand-opening day!

Another fictional fallacy that endeavors to explain the origin of the brand is that Frank and L.E. Phillips, prior to founding the company, had only $66 left when their first successful oil well struck black gold. Because of the timing of their lucky strike, they decided that if they ever marketed gasoline to motorists, it would be christened "Phillips 66." Sounds believable, but it's untrue too. While it's known that the Phillips brothers stretched finances to the limit with their oil explorations, no evidence shows the dollar amount of capital remaining when their Anna Anderson oil well blackened the sky as an Oklahoma gusher.

One exceedingly bizarre tale boasts of high stakes gamblers and luck: According to legend, a Phillips official won the company's first Texas panhandle petroleum refinery in a game of dice! The owner of the facility rolled "double-sixes" in an unlucky toss . . . and lost it all! Back in Bartlesville, company directors liked those unlucky boxcars so much that they named the refinery's product "Phillips 66." A colorful episode, but false. Most likely, this story originates from the oil distillery's infamous neighbor, the 6666 Ranch. Reportedly, the cow corral was won in a poker game with a hand of four sixes!

A few scientifically oriented scenarios have been perpetuated to explain the name too, including the unfounded report that Phillips gasoline was 66 octane and that its much touted "controlled volatility" feature was perfected after 66 lab tests. The truth is, no one knows for sure how many experiments were performed, not even the company. Furthermore, methods for determining gasoline octane wouldn't be adopted until five years after the selection of the original trademark!

The true story of Phillips 66 gasoline begins when the first gallon was offered to motorists in Wichita, Kansas in 1927. Preparations made prior to opening kept corporate employees busy for months. Only a decade old, the company was previously involved only in the production of crude oil. Now, it was venturing into the consumer market for the first time. In the frenzy to perfect its product, selecting an appropriate title to represent their innovative new motor fuel was delayed until the last possible moment!

Still, there was ample time to proclaim one important desire: the name for Phillips' new liquid had to have a hook. A catchy brand identifier stood more chance of garnering the motorists' attention at the pumps. In an effort to meet this criterion, researchers recommended using the benchmark for implying quality in that era, namely "high gravity." Because the new fuel was in the range of 66, it was suggested the numerals be used as a moniker. But, as the choice was logically analyzed, scientists surmised that a colophon linked to one specific gravity wouldn't mesh with Phillips' concept of varying gravity and controlling volatility to fit a range of seasons and locales.

Finally, a special committee was organized for the sole purpose of determining a new trademark. On the night of the meeting, a Phillips official was returning

During the 1930s, oil companies advertised their goods and services in a variety of formats. Phillips distributed colorful movie slides to motion picture palaces across the country to inform theater patrons of their great gasoline. *Courtesy Phillips Petroleum Company*

to the Bartlesville headquarters in a company car—a vehicle being used to road test its new motor fuel. "This car goes like 60 on our new gas!" announced the official. "Sixty nothing," retorted the driver (eye-balling the speedometer), "we're doing 66!" The next day, somebody asked where this dialogue occurred. The answer came back: "Near Tulsa, on Highway 66." Electrified by excitement, the executives took a vote—and finally reached a unanimous decision: Phillips Petroleum would kick off the sale of its powerful new gasoline under the distinctive brand, "Phillips 66"!

Originally introduced to kick off the sale of its first gallon of new gasoline at its inaugural Wichita station, the Phillips 66 trademark is viewed as one of the most widely recognized in America. Many amusing stories and explanations have sprung up over the years attempting to explain the origin of this distinct logo, readily perpetuated by imaginative consumers and those taken to craft romanticized road yarns. While many of these stories are based on fact, others remain mired in myth. Some come across as quite believable, while a handful are crafted in the same vein as fantastic works of fiction. For Frank Phillips, founder of Phillips Petroleum, "66" proved to be an appropriate choice for personalized license plates. Bartlesville, Oklahoma. *Courtesy Phillips Petroleum Company*

Route 66 Motors and General Store is one of today's thriving gift shops doing business along the old alignment of Route 66 (right off I-44 at exit 189, located 1.3 miles east of North Outer Road). Owned and operated by Wayne E. Bales and his wife Patricia, it's stocked with virtually every type of Route 66 memento—including T-shirts, mugs, books, repro signs, auto memorabilia, country accents, and much more. With an adjoining car lot, this dual-function business is a great place to peruse special interest autos and see a variety of vintage advertising signs. It's a must-see stop along the old road. Rolla, Missouri. *Author*

opposite
Migrants who relocated from Oklahoma to New Mexico in the great exodus of the 1930s decided to open up a gas station for their brethren. For all those making their way to the promised land of California, the Oklahoma Service Station was a roadside stop that offered up a little bit of reassurance—and part of the home they had left behind. Oklahoma newspapers, as well as other Oklahoma products, were among the items offered for sale. Questa, New Mexico, Russell Lee photo, 1939. *Library of Congress*

met up with a rest room they didn't like, it was promptly reported to company headquarters back in Bartlesville, Oklahoma.

As news of the Texaco and Phillips units spread along the miles of Route 66, other oil companies began to scrub up their own version of the service station bathroom. For a brief moment in the history of the highway, the cross-country adventurer who desired a carefree comfort stop could count on the impeccable surroundings of the roadside rest rooms. The American gas station had reached its zenith.

By the end of the war, the ability to once again purchase gasoline without restrictions edged out all concern over bathrooms. Once again, Route 66 was flooded with gal-

left
From the Top of the Ozarks to Conway, Missouri, Route 66 had a reputation as being a bloody killer. With more than its share of automobile accidents occurring along that infamous stretch of concrete, the piece of road passing through the town of Devil's Elbow was regarded by many as the "death corner of the world." The Cedar Lodge and Gasoline station was one of Devil's Elbow's more popular places to stop and get refueled. Hooker, Missouri. *Courtesy Chuck Sturm*

In the small towns along Route 66, evidence of yesterday's gas stations is slowly being erased. In the mid-1980s, this downtown gas station in Galena, Kansas, still sported three gasoline pumps and a price signboard. As collectors began to view old pumping equipment and signage with a different eye, scenes such as this became a rarity. Anything and everything that wasn't nailed down was removed, looting the roadsides of much of its legacy and simple treasures. *Jerry McClanahan ©1995*

lons of "go juice" and Americans were getting into their cars in record numbers. In 1949, more than five million passenger cars were manufactured—sold as fast as they could be made to a public eager for postwar luxury. The entire country was off to see the U.S.A. in their

Chevrolets.

Commerce adapted to field the new influx of car customers. Now, instead of driving up to a business, parking, and then walking inside—merchants began catering to the growing obsessions of car culture. Restaurants offered carhops that served cus-

when he opened the nation's first self-service gasoline stations in Los Angeles. These "Gas-A-Terias" consisted of 18 to 21 gasoline pumps set on islands lined up at right angles to the street. In the interest of reducing expenses, station attendants once on duty to check the oil and wipe windows were sacked.

Six girls in tight sweaters raced around the lot in roller skates—much like their satin-clad counterparts at the corner drive-in. Gliding from island to island, they collected money amidst a mad frenzy of vehi-

Selling food and gasoline from one business outlet was the perfect choice for many entrepreneurs setting up shop along Highway 66. With one structure, two demands of travelers could be met with a minimum amount of investment. Near Springfield, Illinois. *Courtesy Jerry Keyser*

tomers in cars and drive-in theaters allowed vehicle owners to watch movies from the front seat. But at the local gasoline station, the effects were quite different: Instead of serving arrivees in their automobiles, customers were urged to pump their own gas! George Urich started the trend in 1947

cles and whirring pumps. The snazzy pump man with bow tie and cap was waiting on the unemployment line. It was a harbinger of things to come.

While the industry tried to dismiss the phenomenon as a dangerous fad, the format held on. By the late 1960s, it was firmly estab-

When cars were less reliable and the population density was lower, the "last chance gas" station poised at the edge of the desert struck fear and loathing into the hearts and minds of the Route 66 adventurer. To prepare themselves for the crossing, customers were warned to fill up their tank with gas, top off the water bag, and buy plenty of provisions. Somewhere in the desert, California. *Shellee Graham ©1995*

lished in the gas station culture of the road and a recognized way of doing business along Route 66. Crazy thing was, hurried customers were getting used to pumping their own gas and really enjoyed the discount prices. The service station attendant's days were numbered.

In the meantime, the Environmental Protection Agency deemed glass containers to be unsafe for gas storage. With great haste, their use

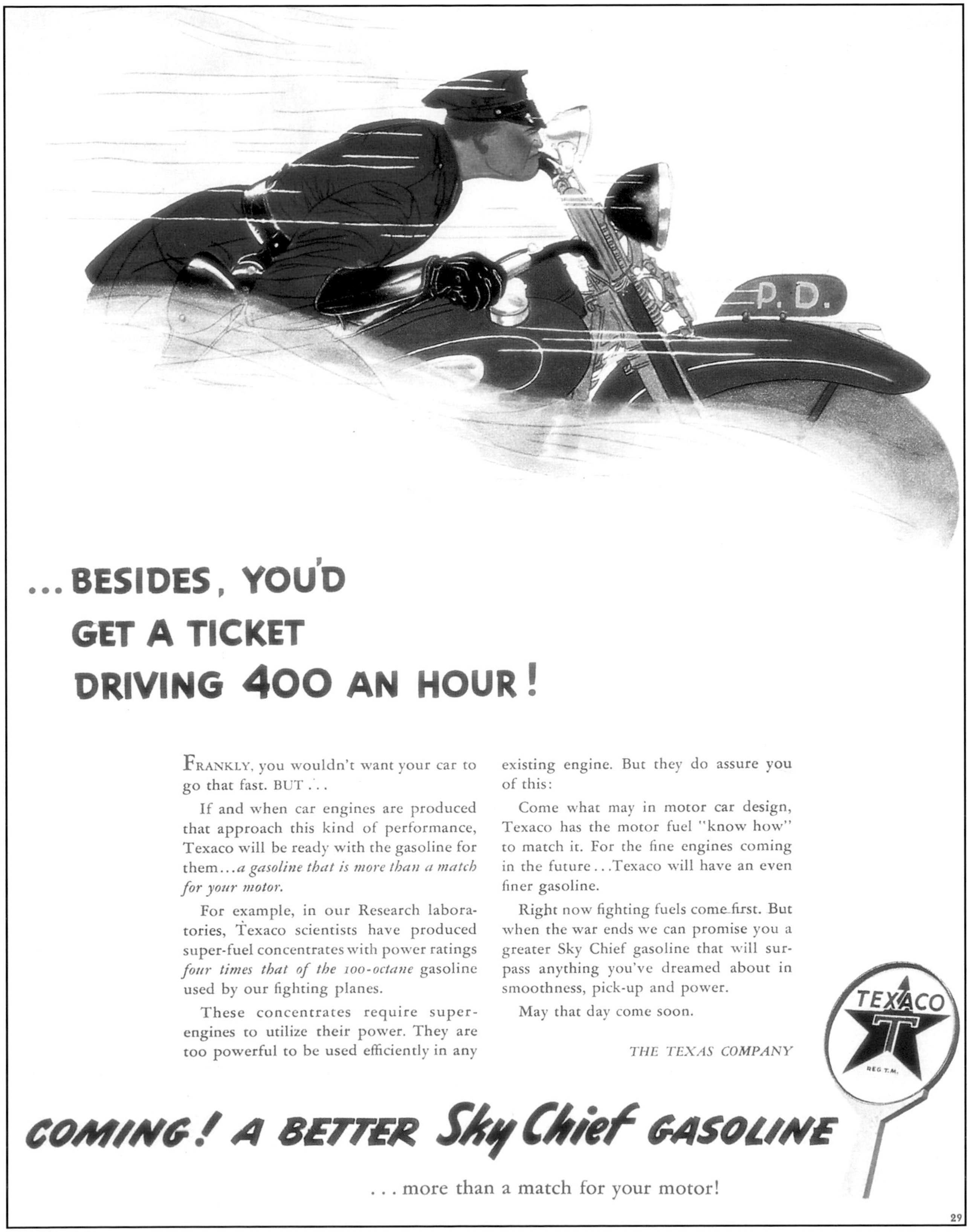
P. D.
...BESIDES, YOU'D GET A TICKET DRIVING 400 AN HOUR!
FRANKLY, you wouldn't want your car to go that fast. BUT . . .
If and when car engines are produced that approach this kind of performance, Texaco will be ready with the gasoline for them...a gasoline that is more than a match for your motor.
For example, in our Research laboratories, Texaco scientists have produced super-fuel concentrates with power ratings four times that of the 100-octane gasoline used by our fighting planes.
These concentrates require super-engines to utilize their power. They are too powerful to be used efficiently in any existing engine. But they do assure you of this:
Come what may in motor car design, Texaco has the motor fuel "know how" to match it. For the fine engines coming in the future...Texaco will have an even finer gasoline.
Right now fighting fuels come first. But when the war ends we can promise you a greater Sky Chief gasoline that will surpass anything you've dreamed about in smoothness, pick-up and power.
May that day come soon.
THE TEXAS COMPANY
TEXACO
T
REG. T.M.
COMING! A BETTER Sky Chief GASOLINE
...more than a match for your motor!
29

opposite below
As commercial architecture, the "house" became a surrogate home for millions of motorized patrons in search of that safe feeling along America's highways. After Pure Oil architect C.A. Petersen found success with his "English-Cottage" design of the mid-1920s, other refiners picked up on the motif. By the close of that decade, residential sites and corner lots were being purchased by many of the large oil concerns in the hopes of constructing new domestic stations. Phillips Petroleum invested heavily in the style with many of their Oklahoma stations on Route 66 embracing the homespun look. Eleventh and Lewis, Tulsa, Oklahoma. *Courtesy Phillips Petroleum Company*

left
By the 1960s, petroleum refiners developed new gasolines on a continual basis, many touting secret chemical additives or revolutionary refining processes. All claimed superior performance and quality, making it difficult for the motorist unschooled in chemistry to discern exactly what was flowing into their car's tank. Texaco introduced the Sky-Chief brand and reinforced its climate-controlled qualities with a series of print ads in national magazines. Specially blended to deliver top performance in each of the 25 weather areas in the country, this "Volatane Control" motor fuel was just the ticket "for quick starts, fast warm-ups, smooth getaways, and power-a-plenty on the highways and up the hills." *Courtesy Texaco Inc.*

The Silent Sentinels of Route 66

"Soon, the silent sentinels of 66 will vanish forever—leaving only faded photographs to validate the hasty evolution of the internal combustion refueling stop."

They stand as lone obelisks along the unused stretches of America's "Mother Road." They sit empty now . . . silent, waiting. The rust and corrosion of the years slowly engulf their exteriors. Like faded billboards, their message has vanished. They are following the hamburger stand and the drive-in theater to extinction. Only a few decaying gas pumps remain. The new wave of superstations has arrived. The era of "wipe the windows and check the oil" has ended.

Today, mini-markets stationed along the interstate have filled the void, offering everything from cheap sunglasses to frozen yogurt. Technology has made it easier for 20th-century motorists to fill their tank, stuff their face, and empty their pocketbooks. The free car wash has become a roadside obsession, and the colors of redesigned petroleum trademarks cast their impersonal glow over the motorways. Like so many other American icons, the filling station has mutated into something unrecognizable.

These days, travelers can look forward to a major consumer project when buying motor fuel along the superslab. First, a search of the general area in and around the parking lot is in order. Where is the pump unit and exactly how does it work? The eager-to-please station attendant canonized during the golden age of motoring is now a legend—and nowhere to be found!

Money-changing pump jockeys now occupy bullet-proof cubicles, isolated from the public. Currency is exchanged through a stainless steel drawer with prepayment after dark. A sophisticated intercom system broadcasts the operator's thanks—a burst of garbled noise abruptly completing the sterile transaction. Afterwards, attempting to use the rest room to wash up is impossible—the door is locked. Toilet paper theft forces the harried customer back to the pay kiosk for the key—attached to a bowling-ball-sized object to prevent its theft!

Remember the days along old Highway 66 when tires where greeted by the familiar "ding-ding" of the driveway air-hose? Those were the days when attendants checked under the hood and attitudes were friendlier. Station employees still had personality then, refining companies a reputation. "A Tiger in Every Tank," the "Flying Red Horse," or "Man with the Star" stirred our imaginations. These were the honeymoon years of America's automotive love affair. Cheap gas with full service! Hubcaps

adorned walls and Greenstamps filled glove compartments. With a friendly ring, gas pumps sounded-off at one-gallon intervals. A visit to the super service station was still a favorite ritual.

Now, only remnants of these classic stations populate the back roads. Many have been converted into used car lots, others just demolished. Usually, a stripped-down pump is all that remains, its removable parts and brand placards cannibalized by overzealous "petroliana" collectors. With only their shells remaining, they echo values from another era, another way of life.

Worn out by a society faithfully served, the aesthetic preferences of former generations permeate every molecule of their structure. With an ethereal character all their own, they decay in glory. Transformed, they measure the advance of time as roadside barometers. The wind, rain, and sun have interacted with their external surfaces causing a transformation. Whether altered by the elements, a well-intentioned station owner with spray paint, or a hammer-wielding vandal, they are windows to another time.

Sometimes, along the forgotten miles of old road—where weeds have grown high and the memories of yesteryear move along the whispering wind—one can almost hear the sounds of old attendants gassing cars. Unfortunately, the recollections grow quieter with every passing year. The surviving relics are slowly

During the 1930s, Ed Edgerton established an outpost along Route 66 at a place in the Black Mountains called Sitgreave's Pass. It started out as a gas station and a cafe, but when the interstate pulled the traffic south, it was transformed into a repository for "stuff." Edgerton worked most of his life as a miner and at one time built a gold-processing mill. In his later years, he gained notoriety when he cured himself of cancer through the use of high temperature and radioactive pads. Rusting visible register pumps are all that remain to remind travelers of the man who discovered "Edgertonite." West of Kingman, Arizona. *Jerry McClanahan © 1995*

being eliminated from America's roadside, replaced by mega-malls, parking garages, and improved freeways. Soon, the silent sentinels of 66 will vanish forever—leaving only faded photographs to validate the hasty evolution of the internal combustion refueling stop.

So look now for the last of the refueling classics that remain. Take a break from the frenzy of the interstate and explore the wonders of the two-lane. The landscape encountered across this mobile America is your museum, the pavement your viewing point. The vehicle you pilot to arrive there is your point of common connection—the transitional link to the consciousness of the road and the generations who constructed it, traveled it, and were born on it.

The major oil refiners didn't miss a trick capitalizing on the success of the visible register pump design. By the end of the 1920s, many began to offer different grades of gasoline dyed with a variety of hues. Texaco sold green gasoline, Esso red, and Sunoco blue. Gilmore promoted their Blue-Green brand of gasoline. Reasoning had it that if normal, uncolored gas sold well, colored mixtures could sell even more. At the same time, a certain sense of mystique could be added to an otherwise mundane commodity. Pie Town, New Mexico, Russell Lee photo, 1940. *Library of Congress*

at filling stations was outlawed. Coincidentally, the majority of mom-and-pop independents unable to afford the latest dispensing equipment relied on the visible register pump (with its glass tank) for their livelihood. Now, restricted by government bureaucracy, the graceful machines that stood as silent sentinels along Highway 66 were just so much scrap metal.

When the so-called oil crisis of the 1970s reduced the flow of gasoline to a trickle, many of the family-run establish-

ments that pumped gasoline along Route 66 dropped from the scene. As fuel supplies were limited by a de facto rationing plan, 5 percent of the 218,000 gas stations in business at the start of 1973 ceased operations. Within this depressed business climate, the major oil refiners wrested the refueling business away from the operators that got it started in the first place.

In the end, only memories of what motor fuel made possible remained: For the farmer fleeing days of dust, it ful-

The Tower Station was opened in Shamrock, Texas, back in April 1936, at the busy intersection of Route 66 and Highway 83 (the Canada-to-Mexico Highway). John Nunn had scratched the design for the building in the dust with a nail. Shamrock businessman J.M. Tindall had a local architect draw up the Art-Deco plans and the station was built. Upon opening, John Nunn and his wife Bebe sponsored a contest to find a catchy name for the new restaurant. A local eight-year-old boy won with the name "U-Drop Inn" and took home a week's worth of waitress pay. T.W. Kines photo, 1948. *National Archives*

If the roadbed is considered to be the soul of Highway 66, it could be argued that the gasoline station is its very heart. From the days of dust bowl flight to modern-day travelers seeking adventure on the open road, the filling station continues to be an important part of the journey. A man can go for six days without water and more than a month without food—but once a gasoline tank is empty, a few feet of forward momentum are all that remain in a powerless automobile. Feeder Road, north of Route 66, Oklahoma. *Author*

filled the promise of the West. For the long-haul trucker, it provided a paycheck at the end of a run. For the traveling salesman off to make a pitch, it was a tool of the trade. Even for the family on vacation, it provided the means to experience a wondrous end. Though some may curse it and others dismiss it, gasoline was the elixir that provided the power to make the motor trip along Highway 66 possible. It was, and always will be, the key to America's Mother Road.

Today's race to get from one part of the country to another in record speed has taken the magic out of travel. Multilane interstates and freeways confine the motorist. Off-ramps and pre-determined exits dictate when and where motorists may eat, sleep, and refuel their gas tanks. Fortunately, alternative corridors such as Route 66 are still thriving. For those that relish the journey and the unexpected sights and sounds a two-lane fandango might bring, America's back roads await. Has the old-time gasoline station faded into obscurity? Not really—life in the fast lane has just foreshortened our view through the windshield, making it difficult to see the few survivors that remain. Chandler, Oklahoma. *Author*

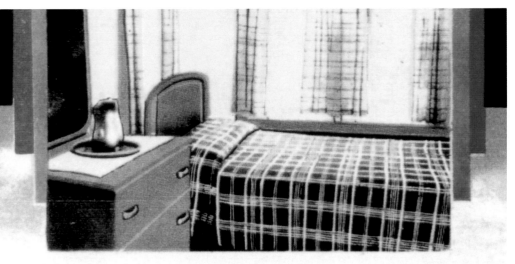

MOTOR INN COURTS
On U. S. 66 - Elk City, Okla.

RECOMMENDED (AAA) MOTOR COURTS

Recommended by the AAA, the Motor Inn Courts featured a full-service Texaco gasoline station in combination with 11 beautifully furnished cabins. Inside, the finest Beauty-Rest mattresses soothed tired backs. They were cool in summer, heated in winter, and even featured hot and cold running water! Their motto? "Where Tired Tourists Meet Good Eats and Good Beds." West Edge of Elk City, Oklahoma. *Courtesy Chuck Sturm*

left
At the road's end in the city of Los Angeles, the gas stations frequented while on Highway 66 were suddenly transformed into colorful visions of neon. Big-city operators spared no expense in their efforts to attract business. Hollywood, California, Russell Lee photo, 1942. *Library of Congress*

Doubling as ambassadors for the company, the Phillips highway hostesses "helped to sell Phillips 66 by their courteous manner, pleasant personalities, and willingness to aid anyone in distress." Cheerfully, they directed tourists to suitable restaurants, hotels, and scenic attractions, as well as took the time to discuss infant hygiene with traveling mothers. Dressed in light blue uniforms and military-style caps, they reminded one of Women's Air Corps recruits. Their white shoes, stockings, and vest pocket handkerchiefs also conjured up images of the local waitress who poured coffee at the neighborhood pancake house. *Courtesy Phillips Petroleum Company*

Certified CLEAN REST ROOMS

In the Route 66 towns of the Arizona desert, gas station owners often fixed prices 2 cents higher than the stations out of town. During the 1950s, the common question was "what have you got in this gas—gold?" At the time, ethyl fuel was almost 42 cents per gallon! The Whiting Brothers chain of stations decided to capitalize on this price gouging by offering gas at a discount. Immense billboards alerting those traveling Highway 66 about upcoming stations were once a common sight along the old road. Continental Divide, New Mexico, 1988. *Jerry McClanahan ©1995*

left

Methods for road building in 1922 relied primarily on manpower and the brute force of animals. This section of the Santa Fe Trail in San Miguel, New Mexico, (from Glorieta to Panchuela) is being surfaced with a layer of crushed rock. When Route 66 was formally commissioned, many sections of roadbed shared a similar design. Until gasoline-powered tractors, graders, and other heavy machinery came into general use, it was slow going for roads in America.
National Archives

HIGHWAY 66

GASOLINE
GREASE
OIL
TIRE
WASH
BATTERY

CAR SERVICE

When the gas rationing of the 1970s concluded, a subsequent contraction of the petroleum industry followed. Many independent stations found it difficult to emerge from the crisis profitably. A large number of these one-shot pumpers were crowded out by the majors and left to fend for themselves in the climate of greater competition. Lacking the financial resources and corporate connections to obtain their share of gasoline, they were in danger. Without gas to sell, bills went unpaid and property was repossessed. Soon, the signs came down and garages were locked until the auctioneer's gavel redirected their fate. Today, a few remnants remain along the back roads of 66 as reminders of the hasty demise of America's "mom and pop" filling stations—a sharp U-turn away from true customer service, simplicity, and the sincerity of a friendly smile. Tijeras Canyon, Albuquerque, New Mexico. *Jerry McClanahan ©1995*

The Flying C Cafe and Gas Station was a Route 66 operation begun by Roy Cline, an Arkie who came to New Mexico during the mid-1920s after he was driven off an Arkansas farm. Cline tried farming, then ran a post office at Ruthern. Later, he bought another spread near the town of Moriarty that was eventually traded for a small hotel in town. He founded the well-known tourist trap known as Clines Corners and through a combination of stubbornness and self-promotion, got the name for his town put on service station road maps. The Flying C was another of his many projects along the old alignment of Route 66. East of Albuquerque, New Mexico. *Courtesy Chuck Sturm*

While many former gas station structures have found new uses in urban areas, those in the outlying regions have had a hard go of it. For the most part, they were abandoned were they stood—making way for the raft of freeway superstations and self-service discount markets assuming dominance over the automobile. Texola, Oklahoma. *D. Jeanene Tiner ©1995*

Grady Jones ran the DX Gasoline station in the town of Arcadia, Oklahoma, for quite a number of years. When he closed down the operation, an impromptu memorial and roadside display of curiosities ensured that his legacy would be remembered. Today, it's one of many service station attractions that draws visitors to the Will Rogers Highway outside of Tulsa. *Author*

In 1905, the Automobile Gasoline Company in St. Louis opened its first "drive-in" filling station featuring a gravity tank and garden hose. Starting primarily in the business as bulk fuel distributors with huge above-ground storage tanks, Harry Grenner and Clem Laessig calculated that their overall volume (and income) could increase by offering gasoline for sale to motorists in a quick, efficient, and practical manner. With the total elimination of the exceedingly impractical method of drum-and-measure refueling, their experiment proved a success. Motorists liked the idea of filling a gasoline tank with a flexible garden hose, and soon the enterprising pair operated about 40 outlets in Missouri, plus a depot. *Courtesy American Petroleum Institute*

chapter three

At the last roadside hot-dog stand you patronized
how clean or otherwise were the dishes, the knives,
the forks, the spoons, the glasses? How clean do you
surmise, were the utensils in which the food had
been cooked? Was there an opalescent skin of soap
or grease on top of the water in your glass? Did you
have an urge to give your coffee spoon a going-over
with your sleeve, handkerchief or napkin while the
lady or gentleman behind the counter wasn't looking? Did you by chance pick up a stomach-ache or a
case of trench mouth at the place?
—"Ptomaine Joe's Place," Collier's, October 1, 1938

Roadside Food:
Dining Out
and
Dining In

During the salad days of the 1950s, Route 66 was a great smorgasbord of regional fare. All along the miles simmered a boundless brunch, an exciting variety of food and beverage that could be sampled at greasy spoons, roadside diners, frantic truck stops, trading-post lunch counters, drive-in dinettes, ramshackle hot dog stands, and elaborate sit-down restaurants.

In Illinois, it was perfectly "normal" to chomp on delicious Steakburgers and gulp Tru-flavor milkshakes. Over in Missouri, Ted Drewes' old-fashioned custard cones put the

Rod's Steak House was started in Williams, Arizona, by Rod Graves and his wife in 1945. At one time, Graves had a Hereford ranch east of Williams. His cattle were branded with his Bar Mary Jane brand, the restaurant's trademark. The eatery itself is located in a long, rather nondescript building that takes up the whole block between Williams and Railroad Avenues. Today, Stella and Lawrence Sanchez own and operate this Route 66 standard and continue to satiate the appetites of all those motorists in search of a real American steak. Williams, Arizona. *Courtesy Chuck Sturm*

left
Along Route 66, Juan Delgadillo and his brother, Angel, have become living legends. While Angel runs a small barbershop in Seligman, Arizona, Juan entertains (and feeds) customers at the Snow Cap Drive-In. Quite the practical joker, he has prepared a number of surprises for unsuspecting patrons. Fortunately, the food is no surprise: It's a classic mix of simple road food served up with speed and style. *Jerry McClanahan ©1995*

Jim's was just one of many eateries along the old road that tried to capitalize on friendly familiarity. Whether it was Bob's Grill, Alice's Restaurant, Joe's Bar and Grill, Rosie's Diner, or Kathy's Cafe, most roadside dining spots had one attribute in common: great customer service. In the days before the impersonal attitudes found at today's fast-food restaurants were accepted as the norm, friendly waitresses, talkative fry cooks, and helpful busboys made dining along the highway a real treat. Vinita, Oklahoma. *Preziosi Postcards*

chill into summer. Meanwhile, the Kansas heartland set the standard for baked breads. Cruising the "Lone Star" state, drivers dined on Texas T-bones as jalepeños tickled taste buds. Across the border, the meals of New Mexico and Arizona set mouths ablaze with savory spices. For dessert, Southern California served up a delight of squeezed citrus—providing a "flavorful" ending to the motor trip.

Inundated with this cornucopia of the highway, it was difficult for the motorist to imagine that just 30 years prior the road was limited in its ability to feed. Back then,

ignored. As the automobile rose to dominance, the petroleum peddlers of the 1920s began to view "edible" fuel as just another aspect of car commerce. With underfed travelers already parked at the pumps, it was only good business to provide them with the victuals they desired.

As a consequence, the sale of "road food" became inextricably linked with the sale of gasoline. The diversification required no great sacrifice, since the bulk of refuelers operating in the rural territories of 66 were often owned by families that lived on site. In these instances, a backroom kitchen and well-stocked larder were the only prerequisites. All one had to do was add a Coca-Cola cooler, make a deal with the iceman, and wait for the hungry to drive in.

It was a marketing plan that worked well for George Morrow, a one-time farmer and retail merchant hailing from Iberia, Missouri. The year was 1932—the very height of the Great Depression—when he decided to start his own refueling business along the nation's most traveled route. With an investment of $1,500, he purchased 3-1/2 acres of frontage on the West Kearney "bypass" and began building his personal vision of a roadside oasis.

Constructed with a veneer of fossilized "worm rock," Morrow's station was planned to serve as both an auto facility and as permanent shelter for his family. The dual-purpose "housestore" was a natural choice for the rural operator planning to prospect the highway for gold: It was inexpensive to build,

car owners had to rely on themselves when it came to refilling the human tank. Between the towns along Highway 66, it was easier to find a gallon of gas than it was to rustle up a square meal.

Even so, the symbolic relationship between food and gas was not one to be

Ed Waldmire Builds a Better Hot Dog

"Although the secret formula for Waldmire's batter casing was patented, clever cooks across the country began developing their own version of the vertical hot dog."

*N*estled between two halves of a fluffy bun and topped with a dollop of mustard, the common frankfurter has been quite content for more than 100 years. The public had universally accepted this format as the norm—that is, until Edward Waldmire came along and decided to turn the wiener world on end—literally—and reinvent the beloved, hand-held comestible most Americans know and love as the hot dog.

This incredible rethinking of a culinary icon began during the early 1940s, when Waldmire was visiting his brother in Muskogee, Oklahoma. There, a hash-slinger working a local greasy spoon flaunted a homemade specialty featuring three wieners cooked in batter! To solidify the eccentric entree, it took 15 minutes of baking in a strange contraption resembling a waffle iron. While lacking points in aesthetics and presentation, the brothers agreed the dish was a flavor combination to remember.

Still, it wasn't until Waldmire was drafted into the military that the possibilities of building a better hot dog were seriously pondered. Stationed in Amarillo, Texas, with the Army Air Corps, his assignment mustering out returning servicemen left him with ample time to think. When an idea popped into his head for a radically new way to prepare tubesteak, he phoned one of his old college buddies, Don Strand (his father ran a bakery in Galesburg, Illinois) and inquired about a special batter concoction with just one important property: The edible formula had to remain stuck to an Oscar Mayer wiener while submerged in the deep fry!

Waldmire received an experimental batch of mix from Strand and proceeded to tinker with various formulations at the base PX. His efforts paid off in 1945 when he emerged triumphant from the kitchen—his vision of a self-contained, great-tasting finger food a practical reality. It didn't take long for the unusual hot-dog-on-a-stick to gain a following with fellow enlisted men bored with the military's unexciting bill-of-fare. Surreptitiously named the "G.I. Hot Dog" by appreciative airmen, it was officially dubbed the "Crusty Cur" by Waldmire.

Upon return to Springfield, Illinois, his wife, Virginia, suggested that he consider a less salacious sobriquet for the fried frankfurter. While Crusty Cur may have scored a direct hit with his Army pals, she felt it was an inappropriate trade name for civilians. After careful deliberation, they agreed on the more appetizing "Cozy Dog." Virginia sketched some preliminary designs for the trademark and refined them into a logo featuring an amorous hot dog duo. They were ready to take the wiener world by storm.

Waldmire organized Cozy Dog Incorporated and in 1946 introduced America's first dipped-dogs to revelers attending the Illinois State Fair. The response was overwhelming and word of the delicious specialty spread countywide.

Encouraged by his popular success at the exposition, Waldmire opened the Cozy Dog House between Fifth and Sixth Streets in Springfield. A year later, he introduced a second eatery across town. By the dawn of the 1950s, car customers were gobbling up so many of the skewered hot dogs that he was inspired to build a third eatery along the Main Street of America. Grand-opening ceremonies for the new Cozy Drive-In commenced on September 10, 1950, with batter-dipped dogs selling for just 15 cents and burgers for 20!

Although the secret formula for Waldmire's batter casing was patented, clever cooks across the country began developing their own version of the vertical hot dog. Whether it be concession operator, theater snack bar, drive-in, or diner—all began to spread news of the savory sausage. The "corn dog" had gone nationwide.

For the next 40 years, Ed Waldmire and his corn-coated creation grew to become a highway

Springfield, Illinois', Cozy Dog Drive-In as it appeared during the 1960s, still featuring the amorous hot dog couple and the great-tasting fast-food dishes developed by founder and Route 66 personality Ed Waldmire. *Courtesy Buz Waldmire*

legend. For motorists passing through Illinois on their way across the great continent, his walk-up drive-in—with its simple menu of home-cooked food and friendly service—became synonymous with good taste. In 1991, his unwavering dedication to food service was recognized with the restaurant's induction into the Illinois Route 66 Hall of Fame. It was a fitting memorial for the inventive Waldmire who took the highway's heavenly off-ramp in 1993.

These days, the Cozy Drive-In and its namesake endures among the fast food franchises doing battle along Springfield's old road. Son Buz and his wife, Sue, perpetuate the legacy by offering the same batter-dipped-dog Ed Waldmire pioneered over one-half century ago. With its future secure, the Cozy Dog remains proof that if you build a better hot dog, the world will truly beat a path—or even a highway—to your door.

Ed Waldmire opened his first Cozy Dog House between Fifth and Sixth Streets in Springfield, Illinois (pictured here). A year later, he introduced another batter-dipped hot dog eatery across town. By the close of the 1940s, customers arriving by car were wolfing down so many of the skewered wieners that he was inspired to build a third drive-in along Highway 66. While today the Cozy Drive-In still serves the same great grub as it did on its grand-opening (1950), the batter-dipped dogs don't sell for 15 cents anymore. Springfield, Missouri. *Courtesy Buz Waldmire*

economical to operate, and allowed for 24 service.

From the road, Morrow's operation looked like almost every other filling depot of the day. Three visible-register fuel dispensers attracted customers with regular, ethyl, and white grades of petrol. But if one looked closer, the domestic clues were everywhere: Between the pumps and the road, a decorative flower box suggested a woman's touch. Behind the store, the family's Guernsey milk cow grazed the pasture.

Inside the structure, two bedrooms, a living room, and a dining area were reserved for the family. In the kitchen, a gasoline stove allowed Morrow's wife, Ethel, to work her craft, mostly preparing simple sandwiches and other short order meals (her culinary skills later earned her a job at the Grove, a restaurant in Springfield). Her home-baked pies enticed motorists to pull up a stool and eat lunch.

And that they did, consuming dinners at the serving table set up near the front window. From this vantage point, customers perused an assortment of goods—including breads, milk (supplied by the bovine out back), and the usual traveling supplies one might need for the open road. Kids drooled at the sight of Baby Ruth and Hershey bars, and their parents opened their wallets to quell the crying.

For its time, the combined grub and gas stop pioneered by the Morrow family was an appropriate way to provide roadside amenities to the Route 66 traveler. But despite its obvious utility, the housestore

Route 66 was the home for countless drive-in restaurants during the 1940s and the 1950s. Unlike the occasional mom-and-pop motels of the same era that occasionally survived the invasion of franchising, the majority of the curb servers were forced out of business. The introduction of the fast-food hamburger and the assembly-line techniques used to make and serve them literally fried the competition. Carhops and window trays were no match for the fast, impersonal, food service of the future. Peach Springs, Arizona. *D. Jeanene Tiner ©1995*

From the earliest days of the internal-combustion engine, truckers, travelers, and other denizens of the highway have relied upon the humble cup of coffee to keep them awake while in transit. Over the years, a variety of restaurants, cafes, diners, and greasy spoons have made a livelihood out of serving up a basic brew. At Formica serving counters across America, "espresso" is a foreign term reserved for shopping centers and strip malls. Albuquerque, New Mexico. *Dan Harlow ©1995*

QUMACHO INN, PEACH SPRINGS, ARIZONA
RESTAURANT AND MODERN MOTEL, INDIAN CURIOS, GIFTS

The Qumacho Inn was one restaurant (with motel out back) that didn't try to disguise itself as something it wasn't. It was simply a cafe—a quick, inexpensive place to get a cup of coffee and a blue-plate special. Even so, it was a Route 66 business that still wanted to stay current with the latest architecture. The circular window installed in the front facade was an obvious attempt to keep up with the craze for streamlining begun during the 1930s. *Courtesy Chuck Sturm*

CHICKEN "66" - ON U.S. 66 AND 75 - TULSA, OKLA.

Of all the restaurant styles begun along the Route 66 Highway, no other kind of eatery was as easy to set up as the chicken stand. During the 1930s, the virtual absence of government regulation and red tape made it easy for grandma to exploit her culinary talents. Unfortunately, the success of the automobile and the commerce created by it spelled the end of the individual operator. The franchised, homogenized chicken shops were destined to take over, relegating homespun outfits like "Chicken 66" to obscurity. Tulsa, Oklahoma. *Courtesy Chuck Sturm*

did not rise to dominate the highway restaurant trade. By the close of the Roaring Twenties, the art of feeding the motorist had already evolved far beyond this limited format. One of the most visible mutations was dubbed the "truck stop."

In 1928, J.P. Walters and his son-in-law John W. Geske stumbled into the truck stop game when they decided to try their hand at the oil business. Their idea was a jobbership to sell refined product to commercial and retail customers. They leased a Route 66 location in McLean, Illinois, and to capitalize on the idea that southern states had the best hospitality, they christened their new building the "Dixie."

After a short while, they realized that the evening hours brought in a whole new set of customers. Unlike the motorist, commercial truck drivers hugged the road all night long—hauling their freight under rigid time restraints. To make the trip, they required gas, oil, and a strong cup of coffee. In order to maximize turnover (and to ensure their success), Geske and company decided to stay open all night.

Before too long, the big rigs became the primary focus. To aid the night time drivers, the Dixie started selling the truckers coffee and sandwiches. As news of the highway

When McDonald's announced in 1967 that is was going to increase the price of its burgers to 18 cents, shock waves rocked the industry (the average price of a burger had remained at 15 cents for years). Blamed on rising beef costs and spiraling expenses, the hike was an ominous precursor to the great burger battles to come. Labeled by the press as "Black Wednesday," the stage was set for the elimination of many smaller chains. After a period of unprecedented growth, the proliferation of the McDonald's hamburger clones was over. The casualties lined Route 66 like so many fallen soldiers. Bridgeton, Missouri. *Shellee Graham ©1995*

hospitality spread, more and more drivers making the run between Chi-town and St. Lou wheeled in for a bite. When the demand for food exceeded the demand for fuel, the menu stretched to include plate lunches. By the time dinner and dessert were added, a wall in the dining room had to be knocked out to accommodate the crowds!

As the 1930s came to a close, business at the Dixie boomed. On an ordinary Saturday night, more than 1,000 visitors jammed the parking lot to fill up fuel tanks and sample the broasted chicken. By then, the specialized truck stop was an established resource of Highway 66 and a dependable place for any traveler to dine.

At the same time America's truck stops and house stores were honing their services, other eateries were emerging in the shadow of the gas pump. By clustering near established businesses geared to the tourist, operators hoped to recruit excess customers. There were more than enough customers for the cafes, diners, and coffee shops to come: by 1949, more than 43 million motor vehicles were whizzing down the nation's highways.

For Harry Tindle, it was the perfect time to get into the roadside restaurant business. His location was Kingman, Arizona—a major stop for motorists crossing the desert into California. Right there on the dusty ribbon of Route 66, he opened a small dining spot in the space adjoining Allen P. Bell's "Flying A" Service Station. It was called the Tideway Cafe.

By the 1960s, the Steak n Shake chain of drive-in restaurants was well-known throughout the Midwest—especially along Route 66. Gus Belt's original formula for serving up a complete meal consisting of Steakburger and a hand-dipped milkshake became the roadside standard. "It's a Meal" was the company's popular slogan. Because the customer could see the order being prepared, "In Sight It Must Be Right" became another car-dining catch-phrase. Webster Grove, Missouri. *Shellee Graham ©1995*

The Rocket Drive-In exists as a hamburger-stand flashback doing business along one of the most nostalgic stretches of the old road. While the juicy, dripping-with-fat hamburgers depicted on their sign are no longer sold for 10 cents, the Rocket's nostalgic atmosphere transports visitors back to a time when carhops zipped around on roller skates and clipped trays full of comfort food on the windows of parked cars. Main Street 66, Afton, Oklahoma. *Author*

Before the McDonald brothers enlisted the services of Ray Kroc to franchise their hamburger stands, they attempted to tackle the task themselves. Of those early burger outlets, this Azusa, California, location was constructed in 1954 and is one of the last extant examples to be found along old Route 66. Architect Stanley Meston and assistant Charles Fish designed the candy-striped structure, but it was Richard McDonald himself who actually came up with the idea of the golden arches. This unit was closed in February 1984. *Jerry McClanahan ©1995*

Like many of the competing restaurants in Kingman, the Tideway was a no-frills diner without tables—customers were provided with nothing more than 14 stools around a small counter. Along with the beverages and carry-out snacks expected by the postwar traveler, the standard road food fare was served.

Bell recalls the complementary arrangement with great fondness: "We worked together . . . somebody would come in and ask where they could get a good sandwich and I would tell them 'right next door.' Somebody would ask Harry where they could get a tire fixed and he would tell them 'right next door!' Yeah, we ran a real good business there, we helped each other out." But it was more than just hype. The Tideway Cafe served up some great food.

"I'll never forget the breakfast" brags Bell. "Boy . . . he had a grill right in front where you could sit and watch him cook—he was sharp! Bacon, eggs, hash browns, toast, coffee—all for one buck!" With all the motels in the area, the traffic was brisk enough to afford Tindle a pink Cadillac and a matching power boat! Both were parked nearby, evidence

98

Robert C. Wian was the brains behind the counter of a 10-stool hamburger stand purchased from two little old ladies in 1936. To raise the money needed to buy this Glendale, California, eatery, he sold his prized 1933 DeSoto. Unfortunately, the sale only netted $300—the women were asking $350! Still, he scraped up the balance and renamed the joint "Bob's Pantry." Then, when local bass player Stewie Strange asked for "something different" one night in 1937, Wian created a new sandwich and made history. The double-deck cheeseburger was an immediate sensation and was later dubbed the "Big Boy," a name inspired by local lad Richard Woodruff. A cartoonist regular sketched the portly kid on a napkin and later, statues of the burger-toting boy became a familiar sight along portions of the old road. 900 Colorado Boulevard, Glendale, California. *Courtesy Richard McLay*

Although the diner has been perceived as a strictly New England phenomenon, rare outposts of this American institution have made their home along Route 66. During the 1930s, Andy's Street Car Grill was the place to get "The Finest Food in the Ozarks." Air conditioning inside the converted streetcar was part of the deal, as well as Andy's limitless hospitality. Note the menu cards at the ceiling edge. Lebanon, Missouri. *Courtesy Chuck Sturm*

of an American dream come true—one built with an ocean of coffee, eggs-over-easy, and a side of hash browns.

Meanwhile, similar dreams materialized along Highway 66. By the early 1950s, a drive-in style that catered to people in their cars rose to become one of the most popular modes for dining. It was a concept that gained notoriety in 1921 when Dallas

mercantile magnate Jessie Kirby convinced physician Reuben Jackson to invest in his idea for a drive-in sandwich stand. His sales pitch: "People with cars are so lazy they don't want to get out of them to eat!"

Their first Texas Pig Stand was built along the busy Dallas-Fort Worth Highway and served up a basic repertoire of barbecue and beverage. Unschooled in the practice of four-wheel dining, commuters passing by eased up on the gas to satisfy their curiosity and to do what the porcine sign board suggested: "Eat a Pig Sandwich!" They weren't disappointed.

Although the food wasn't anything out of the ordinary, nothing could prepare the staid motorist for the Pig Stand's service: When a car drove up to the curb, a young lad jumped up onto the running board before the driver could even come to a complete stop! Clinging to the side, boys clambered on and off to gather their orders. After someone referred to the waiters as "carhops," the craze for curb service was on.

News of just how fun it was to eat in the front seat traveled. As fast as four wheels could carry it, details of the unique drive-in filtered out along the connecting roadways. Within the span of two decades, carhops were serving food throughout most of the Route 66 territories.

For those who revere the golden years of touring food, drive-ins make up the most vivid memories. After all, face-to-face service was the rule of the day. Carhops clad in satin majorette uniforms skated among the cars. Serving trays clipped onto the steering wheel or window and were stacked high with sizzling burgers, golden French fries, and ice cream milkshakes.

In the city of Los Angeles, visitors arriving by way of Route 66 were thrilled by the neon visions lining the boulevards. Out there, most of the drive-ins employed circular architecture to maximize parking and minimize labor. To circumvent local laws barring oversized signs, resourceful restaurateurs mounted elaborate advertising pylons on their rooftops to get attention.

Showman Harry Carpenter erected one of the most ostentatious stands at the intersection of Sunset and Vine in the early 1930s, causing quite a stir for locals. As reported in a 1946 issue of *The Diner*, Carpenter "dressed up this basic idea [drive-in service] with typical Hollywood glitter. He paved his lot, put up a building that looked like a cross between the Taj Mahal and Mary Pickford's swimming pool bath house and found a batch of would-be stars starving to death while waiting for the big chance."

However, the architecture reminiscent of a giant, skewered hamburger was not limited to California. The quest for road food razzle dazzle influenced many of the drive-ins along Route 66. In Tulsa, Bishop's "drivin" emulated the West Coast motif with a multi-layered octagon. Illuminated by spotlights, it appeared as a jewel in the western night. Garland's Oklahoma City eatery had a similar effect: with a massive tower shooting up from its forward bow, neon tubes bathed the parking lot with a warm glow.

continued on page 104

In 1940, the McDonald brothers sliced their "Airdrome" orange juice stand located in Arcadia, California, in two pieces and transported it to a new site at Fourteenth and E Streets in San Bernardino, California. It was remodeled, reorganized, and outfitted with a bevy of 20 carhops in satin uniforms. On weekend nights, 125 cars jockeyed for position in the parking lot! *Courtesy Richard McDonald*

Spencer Groff Unearthed a Roadside Diamond

"Groff realized that if he could figure out what these pleasure-bound excursionists needed, he could eke out a living—right in his own front yard."

At the turn of the century, Spencer Groff left the family farm in Villa Ridge, Missouri, to pursue his dream of becoming an attorney. His studies were cut short, however, when speculation on the St. Louis Mercantile Exchange led to financial ruin. Using the old homestead as collateral, he returned home broke—determined to somehow pay back the accumulated debt.

Fortunately, the two dirt paths that ran alongside his acreage on Altamont Hill brought the promise of new fortune. Sputtering motorcars now speeded past on roads previously occupied by covered wagon, stagecoach, and buggy. Groff realized that if he could figure out what these pleasure-bound excursionists needed, he could eke out a living—right in his own front yard. Plums from the orchard became his first product, an item that sold out on a busy Labor Day weekend. He was in business!

Bolstered by the success of his first retail endeavor, he decided to turn over the profits and buy a supply of soda pop. An old washtub with ice held the bottles beneath a tattered umbrella planted near the shoulder. As the hot summer temperatures created thirst, he and his helper, Mack, exchanged colas for coins and established their presence along the roadway. When the weather turned frigid, sales dropped dramatically and plans

Known as "The Old Reliable Eating Place," The Diamonds was one of the most visited restaurants along Highway 66. Located at the junction of U.S. Highways 50, 66, and Missouri 100, it had a location that would be the envy of any restauranteur. Former busboy Louis B. Eckelkamp (he started there in 1933) took over the operation from founder Spencer Groff and turned it into a roadside travel center of renown. In the early 1960s, he rebuilt the old Diamonds destroyed by fire (shown) at the cost of $350,000 and reopened it as a combination restaurant, cafeteria, coffee shop, curio shop, bus ticket office, travel bureau, popcorn stand, and filling station. Villa Ridge, Missouri. *Preziosi Postcards*

soon the aroma of homemade pies filled the air. The year was 1923 when the little store at the crossroads became a recognized fixture.

Still, Groff's neighbors were skeptical of the eclectic stand. They perceived it as a whim, unaware that it represented his sole income and relief from debt. It had a similar effect on customers: One day, a highway official stopping in for a drink commented that the ramshackle gazebo reminded him of nothing more than "Adam's Banana Stand!" Amused more than insulted, Groff pondered the significance and decided to capitalize on the curious observation.

So, without any formal blueprints or specifications—there in the dust to which he had bowed in defeat—he measured off a diamond of undreamed value. Using a pick ax, he scratched out the rough outline of a what was to become a new building, aligning it with the fork in the road, with two sides paralleling the highways. Before the first nail was struck, an appropriate exterior was already in mind: White clapboard—painted with big bunches of bananas!

Even this new structure was eventually outgrown. As the talk of highways became a serious fact in the state capitol at Jefferson City, traffic at the junction grew. Within months, the new Banana Stand was surrounded by concrete ribbons. Motorists visited in numbers like never before, and of course, Groff was ready. He was dreaming of his greatest gem of all—a full-service restaurant dedicated to delicious dinners and service. On "road opening day," July 3, 1927, he greeted the world with his finest jewel. It was called "The Diamonds."

were formulated for a much grander stand that could operate year around.

When spring arrived, Groff was ready: He planted four posts into the ground and topped them with a dilapidated roof from an old grain silo. Boards were nailed to the sides to form an enclosure and a small stove brought inside to provide heat during winter. A small railing was installed around the perimeter of the hut to keep customers at bay. Inside, tobacco, gloves, overshoes, overalls, gingham shirts, and socks lined the shelves. Outside, a fuel dispenser was installed so that the depleted tanks of automobiles could be refilled with gasoline.

By that time, the farm was once again producing edibles, so it seemed only natural to offer food to customers. The main course became none other than Frankfurter sandwiches, supplemented by fresh, chilled buttermilk at five cents a glass. Vegetables from the garden were harvested for sale and fruits used for delectable pastries. Groff's sister, Ursula, joined the endeavor and

News of "The Old Reliable Place" spread by word of mouth and soon it became a favorite stop for bus companies, soldiers on their way to Fort Leonard Wood, and an endless procession of hungry sight-seers. Celebrities often popped in. On Sundays and holidays, the walls seemed to bulge with customers who came to taste the famous food. With every blue-plate special served, Groff's tremendous debt dwindled away.

In the end, it could be stated that Spencer Groff stumbled upon his life's work right outside his front door. Through a combination of faith, luck, and patience, he turned an ordinary fruit stand into one of the most memorable landmarks along the Mother Road. For him, all it took was a little time—and effort—to uncover the most valuable diamond of them all.

THE DIAMONDS RESTAURANT AND CABINS

JUNCTION 50·66·100   VILLA RIDGE, MO.

The motto at the Diamonds was "Service is First, Courtesy Always." The ultramodern (for the 1960s), California-streamlined building was designed by architect Frank Hayden and constructed by Oliver L. Taetz, general contractor. The fire-proof structure covers a half acre and features a concrete foundation and a brick exterior. Villa Ridge, Missouri. *Courtesy Chuck Sturm*

After opening his roadside refreshment stand, neighbors began to wonder about the strange course Spencer Groff had taken. They looked upon the stand as a whim, not knowing it represented his sole income and path out of debt. He ignored their comments and hoped that one day his stand and the surrounding knoll would be called Altamont Park (after his old school). He had visions of Sunday afternoons with cars parked four deep for service and even erected a sign on the old building nearby with the title "Altamont Park." One day, fate stepped in when a highway official stopped for a drink and commented that the place reminded him of nothing more than "Adam's Banana Stand." Finally, Spencer Groff's Route 66 stand had a name. Villa Ridge, Missouri. *Author*

The Diamonds is a Route 66 landmark to this day. However, it's not the original structure built by Spencer Groff and rebuilt (it was destroyed in a 1949 fire) by Lewis Eckelkamp. During the 1960s, Highway 66 was moved when I-44 came through. Eager to remain near the traffic, the Eckelkamp management decided to abandon the Diamonds and construct a new structure at the end of the freeway's access ramp (two miles away). At the same time, the path of the highway shifted from the Franklin County ridgetop, it

encroached on the Tri-County Truck Stop in Sullivan, Missouri. Owners Arla and Roscoe Reed were forced to shut down and began looking for a new business home. After they rediscovered the Diamonds, it was refurbished, cleaned, and polished. In 1971, they moved in and the old yellow brick Diamonds building was reborn as the Tri-County Truck Stop. (Behind little girl: Spencer Groff, right; Lewis Eckelkamp, left). Villa Ridge, Missouri. *Courtesy Ralph Bay*

Along the old road, local hangouts and other undiscovered eateries remain an untapped resource for automotive explorers. Routinely, present-day Route 66 adventurers pass them by. While the standard dining venues have received more than their fare share of press, the mom-and-pop cafes, neighborhood beer joints, honky-tonks, and other rustic bar and grills seem content just to be themselves. On the Kansas/Missouri Border. *Author*

continued from page 102

Unfortunately, the average restaurant owner who managed to weather the Depression had little capital left for upgrading architecture. As a result, the focus of many eateries became the food. Some cafes made a deal to sell the ever-popular "Chicken in the Rough," while others concentrated on improving the hot dog. To the delight of highway travelers, specialized dishes and original entrees ruled the day.

Along Illinois 66 in Normal, A.H. "Gus" Belt took over the old Shell Inn after the Depression and converted it to a neighborhood tavern. He sold chicken dinners and experimented in the kitchen, testing a greaseless grill for cooking up ground steak. When the town enacted a "no liquor" law, he

made plans to convert the cafe into a burger bar and dropped beer in favor of hand-dipped shakes. By 1934, he perfected the "Steakburger," a ground beef sandwich fortified with cuts of T-bone, strip, and sirloin.

Armed with a sure road food winner, Belt introduced "Steak n Shake" restaurants to the Illinois motorist. Car customers responded enthusiastically to the four-way service known as "Takhomasak" (take home a sack) and came to trust the gleaming, white drive-ins as reliable rest stops. With food orders made where patrons could see them, "In Sight, It Must Be Right" became the creed for other greasy spoons to copy.

Nearly 1,700 miles west—at the opposite end of Highway 66—Richard and

Maurice "Mac" McDonald were preparing to conduct some food experimentation of their own. While struggling to make a movie theater called the Beacon profitable, they noticed that a local hot dog vendor was attracting a remarkable amount of business. Realizing that they might be in the wrong line of work, they decided to open their own stand. It was 1937, and money was tight.

As luck would have it, they learned that a local Sunkist packer was selling bruised fruit at a bargain. So, they made a sweet deal to buy twenty-dozen oranges for a quarter, borrowed money from a local bank, and went to work. Using borrowed lumber, they erected a gazebo along Arcadia's Huntington Drive (Route 66). On top, they crowned it with a large replica of an orange juice drink. Since Monrovia's airport was nearby, they called it the "Airdrome."

When the McDonalds learned how much demand there was for fresh-squeezed juice, they opened a second stand right across the street! To impress the thirsty travelers driving in from Needles and the Arizona desert, they

crafted the edifice to look like a piece of fruit. During the summer months, motorists by the hundreds stopped off to down an icy chalice of juice and to take snapshots of the orange-shaped hut.

Bolstered by the resounding success of their refreshment stands, the McDonalds decided to enter into the drive-in

The Big Texan Steak Ranch is one of those stops along Route 66 to be made on an empty stomach. Why? If you can finish their famous 72-ounce steak (along with all the side dishes and trimmings that come with it), it's free! Hopefuls may not leave the table once they have begun and may leave the fat behind (to be judged by the management). The restaurant was originally located on Amarillo Boulevard but was relocated by the owners when the interstate cut off business in 1968. Presently, it occupies a site along Interstate 40. Amarillo, Texas. *Dan Harlow ©1995*

Featuring an octagonal layout and
massive advertising pylon jutting
from its rooftop, Bishop's Driv-Inn
was once a roadside gem. Located
on Highways 66 and 44 in Tulsa,
Oklahoma, it was a classic example of the circular carhop eateries
popularized in Southern California
during the 1930s and 1940s. *Courtesy Chuck Sturm*

below
The Boots drive-in featured the
classic styling of Streamline Moderne architecture complete with
wraparound windows and side-
mounted portholes. Twin canvas
canopies provided protection
from the elements and multiple
Coca-Cola buttons the perfect
complement for colorful paint.
Positioned at the busy junction of
U.S. Highways 66 and 71, its souvenir shop was always ready with
inexpensive trinkets. Carthage,
Missouri. *Courtesy Chuck Sturm*

opposite
Many drive-in restaurants located
on the busy cross streets of Los
Angeles were considered "taxpay-
ers." Never intended to become
permanent landmarks, they typically operated for a short life span
of 10 years or less. As real estate
values of these prominent plots
rose, the buildings that occupied
the space could no longer support
the value of the land. During the
1950s, restauranteur Stanley
Burke bought out all of the
remaining Simon's units and converted them to Stan's drive-ins.
Eventually, none of the operations
survived. Classics like Simon's
were memories when high-rise
towers and shopping malls took
over the streetside territory. *Security Pacific National Bank Photograph
Collection/Los Angeles Public Library*

You'll come to
Bishop's

Bishop's Driv-Inn

You'll return to
Bishop's

SEATING CAPACITY 156

10th and Boston

ON HIGHWAYS 66 AND 44

TULSA, OKLAHOMA

Boots Drive-in & Gift Shop
At the Crossroads of America
Junctions U. S. 66 - 71 Carthage, Mo.

business with full force. In 1940, they sold the oversized orange stand and sliced the Airdrome in two. It was moved to a new location at Fourteenth and E Street in nearby San Bernardino where workers enlarged, remodeled, then carefully reassembled it.

Richard McDonald introduced "Speedy" as their mascot and installed a neon sign featuring the blinking chef roadside. Inside, a

Located on the busy stretch of Central Avenue in Albuquerque, New Mexico, the El Sombrero Drive-In was the quintessential blend of object and architecture along Route 66. For a drive-in restaurant of circular design, a sombrero provided the perfect format for the display of rooftop neon, brim-side advertising, and protection from the rays of the sun. Could there have been any question from those driving past as to what kind of food was served here? *Preziosi Postcards*

grill cook made up hamburgers, hot dogs, and barbecue plates. Out on the parking lot, twenty carhops donning satin uniforms handled the crowds of customers: during weekend nights, 125 vehicles caused a curb service traffic jam! By 1948, their revenues topped the $200,000 mark.

Despite the overwhelming success, the McDonald brothers grew restless. After

World War II they could sense that customers were growing impatient with carhop service. On a hunch, they decided to fire all the hops, pare down the menu, dump the dishes, and store the silver. Three months later, they reopened with a limited menu and a new style of service: At tiny walk-up windows, customers were required to make and carry off their own food orders!

I'll Gladly Be Fried for Chicken in the Rough

"In 1937, their unique grill was patented and the soon-to-be famous rooster trademark registered—
signifying the arrival of America's first franchised food."

For more than 60 years, a specialty platter known as "Chicken in The Rough" has satiated appetites at table-service restaurants, carhop drive-ins, motel dining rooms, and nightclubs along Route 66. Consisting of half a golden brown chicken served with a side of shoe-string potatoes, hot buttered biscuits, and jug 'o honey, it was the ultimate—and tastiest—entree to emerge from the kitchens of the old road.

It all began in 1921 with fledgling restaurateurs Beverly and Rubye Osborne. As legend has it, they borrowed 15 dollars from their milkman, hocked Rubye's engagement ring, and sold the family car—just to scrape up the down payment on a modest, six-stool dinette in Oklahoma City. They packed the tiny eatery on 209 West Grand by offering 19-cent meals and perfecting their secret recipe for pancakes! As profits piled up, the enterprising duo purchased another out-fit—a little drive-in on 2429 North Lincoln, right along the original alignment of the Will Rogers Highway.

By 1936, they were both ready for a vacation and began motoring out to the Golden State. Along the way Beverly hit a pothole, causing Rubye to dump a lunch-box full of chicken to the floorboards. As battered breasts and drumsticks were picked up, she remarked, "This is really chicken in the rough!" The spontaneous comment clicked with Beverly and set his imagination to sizzle. By the time they returned home, plans were made to create a radically new dish based on Rubye's observation.

At first, the Osbornes fried up the unjointed birds "pan style" since they believed it was the only method of cooking that would bring out the true flavor. Unfortunately, it was slow and tedious. As popular demand for the new poultry plat-ter swelled to over 1,500 orders per day, it became apparent that a faster and more efficient preparation method was required. So, Beverly collaborated with a local machine shop owner and proceeded to devise a shallow-pit griddle designed to cook with minimal grease.

The resulting brazier was a specialized unit featuring "built-in" burners for even heat distribution. A shallow slope allowed the fryers to be submerged only half way—regardless of their thickness. Simultaneously, the clever cookplate both pan fried and steamed the pullets to perfection. With a capacity for preparing 30 orders (150 pieces) at one time, it afforded the production-line cooking method necessary to turn a profit—without sacrificing the "home-style" flavor the Osbornes had so beautifully perfected with their single stovetop fry pan.

In 1937, their unique grill was patented and the soon-to-be famous rooster trademark registered—signifying the arrival of America's first franchised food. A mar-keting plan was hatched, spreading the culinary delights of Chicken in The Rough to numerous venues along 66. Among the earliest eateries to pluck the opportunity were Abbot's Cafe in Berwyn, Daniel's Duck Inn at Joplin, Elliott's Court Cafe of Albu-querque, and Kingman's Lockwood Cafe. Oklahoma grew to seven outlets, the orig-inal expanding from four booths and nine stools to a behemoth with 1,100 seats. After Shamrock's U-Drop-Inn and Galena's Tivoli signed up, "I'll Gladly be Fried for Chicken in The Rough!" became one of the most remembered slogans for car cus-tomers along the historic highway.

By 1958, the Osborne's hands-on approach to chicken had spread all the way to the road's end. In California, the drive-in craze was reaching its zenith and shrewd operators were trying everything to make a buck. Los Angeles landmarks like Hen-rys, Carpenter's, and McDonnell's added the unjointed entree to infuse their burger-based menus with variety. The car crowd responded with salivating mouths and open wallets and it wasn't long before the Osbornes were overseeing 156 loca-tions—some as far away as Hawaii and South Africa!

During the 1920s and 1930s, etiquette expert Emily Post proclaimed that every fried chicken dish should be consumed with a knife and a fork. Fortunately, Bev-erly and Rubye Osborne disagreed with this restrained opinion and served up their hand-eaten poultry entree without restraint. Known in the trade as "Chicken in the Rough," the couple's culinary creation became a franchised delight up and down 66. People loved the homey platter consisting of half a fried chicken with side of shoestring potatoes, rolls, and "pot o' honey." **Oklahoma City, Oklahoma.** *Courtesy Chuck Sturm*

Eventually, the franchising of America and the rise of the fast-food industry overtook the Osborne's famous recipe. In 1974, rights to the process were sold to Randy Shaw, an early partner. He subsequently purchased the remaining restaurants in Oklahoma City and continues to manage day-to-day operations at Beverly's Pancake Corner—one of the original locations still extant along the Northwest Expressway.

Today, Route 66 "roadies" may still enjoy the original Chicken in the Rough their parents (and grandparents) smacked their lips for during the early days. It's still eaten the very same way—with a hearty appetite, no silverware, and plenty of nap-kins. Sometimes, the tastes of the past do survive the present—and for that—we may all cluck quietly with delight.

For motorists on a budget, dining along Highway 66 often meant an impromptu running-board picnic. Anything and everything that could be taken along in an automobile was consumed, including fried chicken brought from home. When finances allowed, a visit to a Chicken in the Rough franchise was the next best thing to mama's frying pan. Russell Lee photo, circa 1930s. *Library of Congress*

Accustomed to drive-in dining, the local teenagers didn't take kindly to the new "speedy service system." On Friday nights, the lot was conspicuously absent of hot rods. The carhops cruised by to heckle, informing Dick and Mac that they had their uniforms ready. Worried that they might have made a big mistake, the McDonalds almost switched back the format.

Three months later, their patience was rewarded. Suddenly, the travelers traipsing in from Highway 66 began making regular stops—along with taxi cab drivers, sales clerks, construction workers, and door-to-door salesmen. A diverse clientele discovered that assembly-line cooking translated into fast service and 15 cent hamburgers. As an added bonus, there were no carhops to tip!

"Sometimes we'd have over 100 people in line," remembers McDonald. "But—if we waited until they got up to the window to find out if they wanted a milkshake—the line would have snaked to Los Angeles!" To satisfy the demand, shakes were mixed in advance and stored in a freezer. Two single-shaft, Hamilton Beach mixers were in constant use, occasionally burning out from the stress.

When Ray Kroc, ever-eager representative for the Prince Castle Sales division received an order for ten heavy-duty "Multimixers," he was dumbfounded. Why would one hamburger stand need so many five-spindle mixing units? Filled with curiosity, he got into his car, pulled out onto Highway 66, and pointed his hood toward San Bernardino, California.

CHEESE - After Dinner Portions (Toasted Crackers)

Roquefort 25c	Camembert 25c	Imported Swiss 25c
American 15c	Cream Cheese 15c	Pimento Cheese 15c
Cottage Cheese 15c	Philadelphia Cream 25c	Limburger 20c

SANDWICHES

We Use Our Large Sandwich Bread — Making a Large Sandwich

Cold Pork Sandwich 15c	Bacon and Tomato 20c	Toasted Cheese 15c
Cold Beef Sandwich 15c	Oyster Sandwich 25c	Melted Cheese 30c
American Cheese 15c	Tuna Fish, Mayonnaise 20c	Roquefort Cheese 25c
Sausage Sandwich 15c	Baked Ham 20c	Jelly Sandwich 10c
Cold Ham 15c	Fried Ham 15c	Fish Sandwich 25c
Tongue Sandwich 15c	Olive Nut 20c	Ham and Egg 25c
Pimento Cheese 15c	Chicken Salad 20c	Liverwurst 15c
Lettuce Mayonnaise 10c	Bread and Butter 10c	Deviled Ham 20c
Lettuce Tomato 15c	Cold Chicken 25c	Pineapple Cheese 20c
Hamburger 15c	Sardine Sandwich 15c	Cold Turkey & Mayonnaise 30c
Salisbury Sandwich 15c	Bacon and Egg 25c	Relish Spread 15c
Gooseliver Sandwich 15c	Imported Swiss Cheese 25c	Deviled Egg 15c
Fried Egg 15c	Stuffed Olive 25c	Philadelphia Cream
Peanut Butter 10c	Caviar, Chopped Onion 50c	Cheese 20c
Hard Boiled Egg 15c	Denver on Toast 30c	Imported Salami 15c

HOT SANDWICHES With Potatoes and Gravy - Open Face

Hot Beef or Pork 25c	Hot Roast Veal 25c	Hot Turkey 35c
Hot Roast Lamb 25c	Hot Chicken 30c	Hot Ham 25c

Any Sandwich you do not see we will prepare it on request.

FOUNTAIN SPECIALS

ICE CREAM

Vanilla or Chocolate	
Plain 10c	
Sherbet 10c	
Sundaes all Flavors 15c	
All Sundaes with Nuts 20c	
Bittersweet 15c	
Banana Split 25c	
Parfaits, all flavors 20c	

Hot Fudge Sundae 15c	
Ice Cream Sodas	
All Flavors 15c	
Malted Milk all flavors 15c	
Double Thick Malted	
Milks 20c	
Malted Milk with Egg 20c	
Chocolate Milk 05c	
with Float 10c	

BEVERAGES

Coca Cola 05c	
Root Beer 05c	
Fresh Orangeade 10c	
Fresh Limeade 10c	
Fresh Lemonade 10c	
Lime Rickey 10c	
Ginger Ale per glass 10c	
Bottle Sodas, all flavors 05c	

Whipped Cream Used in all our Fountain Service.   Our Fountain Service is Complete

We will be glad to make any Fountain Special for the Asking

DESSERTS, Pies Cakes and Pastry Made on Premises

Home Baked Pies, per cut 10c	Doughnuts, two for 05c	
Layer Cake per slice 10c	Sweet Rolls, 2 for 05c	
Danish or French Pastry "Home Baked" 10c	Cheese on Pie, Extra 05c	
Fruit Cake 15c	Fruit Jello, plain 10c	
Cookies, two for 05c	with Whipped Cream 15c	

Pie or Cake Topped with Ice Cream 5c Extra; with Whipped Cream 10c

HOT AND COLD BEVERAGES

*Coffee is richest and best when made immediately after the freshly roasted bean
is broken. Court Cafe Coffee is therefore ground only as used — just before it goes
into the big urn. You get all the flavor and goodness of good coffee in every cup.
Blenders of Our Own Coffee.*

Coffee per Cup 05c	Sweet Milk Individual Bottle 05c	
Buttermilk, Individual Bottle 05c	Instant Postum per cup 05c	
Ovaltine, Hot or Cold 15c	Iced Coffee or Iced Tea 05c	
	Cocoa ....10c with Whipped Cream 15c	
	Hot Chocolate ....10c with Whipped Cream 15c	
	Green or Black Tea per Pot 10c	

*Our Own Soft Water Well Furnishes The Softest
Water in the City.*

It is Pure Take Home All You Like.

Court Cafe

ALBUQUERQUE, NEW MEXICO

A La Carte Menu

Be Sure to See

The extra day you spend in Albuquerque will reward you with never-to-be forgotten experiences. Example, the breath-taking "Rim Drive," which takes you through interesting, primitive Tijeras Canyon to the crest of the steep Sandias east of the city. There, 11,000 feet above sea level, and 6,000 feet above the valey, your eyes sweep a hundred-mile view, with Albuquerque lying in the center, like a tiny, flattened ant hill.

West of the city, an easy drive, you find a group of extinct volcanoes. Over beyond, in the Rio Puerco valley, plenty of agate and other unusual rocks.

South thirteen miles you visit the Indian village of Isleta, which was there when Coronado came in 1540, and carries on its communal life today very much as it did then.

Stay another day in Albuquerque—take home life-long memories.

Our Curio and Gift Shop

Don't fail to visit this finely stocked department of the Court Cafe. In order to provide you with all that is unique and worth while in Southwestern curios, Indian jewelry, Indian pottery and basket work, imported Mexican novelties, wares and handicrafts, we have established this shop. The space is small but the choice is extensive, as you will see when you look through its glass cases and open displays.

We are careful to keep the prices down to popular levels. Many local people find it an ideal place to purchase bridge prizes and other small personal gifts to send away. Before you go out, be sure to see what there is of interest for you in our curio and gift department.

Blue Room

This is our cocktail lounge, bar and dispensary. Try its comfortable chairs, its quick, accurate service. Drop in after the theatre, dance or party.

SOUVENIR MENUS

Our Menus make an interesting souvenir of your trip through Albuquerque. We have provided Mailing envelopes to send them home in. PLEASE ask Cashier for one if you wish, but DO NOT take this one.

(Photo captions on the Court Cafe montage: GRAND CANYON, MISSION CHURCH, NAVAJO CHURCH, THE MONUMENTS CANYON DE CHELLEY, KID CARSON'S CAVE, INDIAN WOMAN, WINDOW ROCK, GOVERNOR'S HOUSE INDIAN PUEBLO, TAOS INDIAN PUEBLO)

Upon arrival, Kroc couldn't believe what he saw: at each of the order windows, lines of people were waiting to purchase food. In all his miles of travel, he had never witnessed anything like it. Then and there, he made up his mind that he would become part of the operation. As it turned out, he got his wish: The McDonalds hired him as their franchise agent and within ten years, he spread the

left
In the fall of 1948, the McDonald brothers closed down their San Bernardino, California, drive-in and fired all of their carhops! After a brief shutdown, they reopened with a new food serving plan based on what they called the "Speedy Service System." Its main features were self-service, minimal choice, and fast turnover. The 15 cent hamburger stand—and the American fast food industry—were born! *Courtesy Richard McDonald*

In 1949, Nash promoted its latest automotive model to the American family with images of recreation and comfort. With twin convertible beds and a more-than-roomy interior, Nash's latest offering appeared to be the perfect vehicle for the family eager to take to the roadways and venture into the great outdoors. With the latest Nash, motoring down Route 66 was a highway dream. *Reprinted with permission of the American Automobile Mfg. Assoc.*

fast-food gospel of the burger, fries, and Coca-Cola nationwide.

By the mid-1960s, people traveling down Route 66 couldn't drive very far without seeing those golden arches. Competitors cloned the concept and soon, sprawling cities and their suburbs were brimming with franchised food.

As more and more sections of two-lane 66 were bypassed by new routes, hamburger bars with styrofoamed foodstuffs and plastic utensils vied for position at the freeway exits and access. For those devoted to life in the slow lane, it appeared that the variety of eateries that made up the two-lane were in danger of extinction. The future of road food—or so it was thought— would be devoid of home-style food.

Meanwhile, a great number of restaurants settled in for the duration. With time on their side— they watched as freeways, turnpikes, and interstate highways soaked up customers. Many could not endure the onslaught and died out.

Then, something wonderful bloomed: Route 66 evolved into a certifiable artifact—an oddity, an aberration, a destination in itself. Modern automobilists began to rediscover the dining spots spoken so highly of

Roadside businesses along Route 66 have to change at a moment's notice. They may start out as a dining cafe and when economic conditions change, transform into an automotive repair shop. Passing motorists seldom notice the change until years later when advertising signs begin their slow fade. It's not at all unusual too see the various iterations a business has gone through once the layers of peeling paint reveal the truth: Mom's Cafe or Tire Repair? Riverton, Kansas. *Author*

Hoyt's Highway 66 restaurant featured famous foods that garnered the approval of Duncan Hines. For early restaurateurs, earning the Duncan Hines seal of approval equated to guaranteed success. Hines started out in the restaurant review business by a fortunate stroke of fate. A well-traveled salesman, he had compiled a list of favorite eateries for his friends and family. The public's interest prompted Hines to expand the list and publish it as a book, entitled *Adventures in Good Eating.* By 1939, it was selling at a steady clip of 100,000 per year! Albuquerque, New Mexico. *Courtesy Chuck Sturm*

Route 66 road rumors have it that the Club Cafe made famous by Ron Chavez might reopen. Currently closed and out of business, the restaurant was at one time billed as an "original Route 66 Restaurant since 1935." For years, the smiling mascot known affectionately as the "Fatman" caught the eyes of hungry travelers driving down Route 66. Sadly, after Ladybird Johnson implemented her plans for "Highway beautification," (the grinning Fatman and the billboards he brought to life became few and far between. Santa Rosa, New Mexico, 1983. *Jerry McClanahan ©1995*

by their parents! Hidden for so many years in the eddies and whorls of the forgotten road, classic restaurants were once again in great demand.

Today, the eateries found along America's Main Street have become classics. For all those traveling the old road, standards like the Snow Cap, the Club Cafe, the Cozy Drive-In, Rod's Steakhouse, Pop Hicks, the Dell Rhea Chicken Basket, Barney's Beanery, and the U Drop Inn have come to signify the old road's flavor. They are the pit stops that make up a tasty motor trip. Because—no matter how you bake, boil, fry, or microwave it—Route 66 motorists still travel on their stomachs.

Those Dreaded Days of Desert Water Bags

"When draped outside of a window, slung over the hood ornament, or hung on the side-mounted spare, air rushing over their exterior created an effect likened to 'wind chill.'"

For the traveler trekking across America during the 1920s and 1930s, transportation by car was rife with problems. Tires went flat regularly, if they didn't blow out! Engines threw rods, transmissions seized, and crankcases cracked. But, nothing inspired more dread than a plume of steam billowing from a screaming-hot radiator.

There was good reason: Radiators of the era were often delicate and frequently underrated for their applications. They were quick to overheat in traffic, during hot weather, and on steep inclines. The most inefficient designs even exhibited thermal problems under marginal circumstances, especially if a wad of leaves or splash of mud restricted their air flow. Certain automobiles of the age like the Wasp phaeton (with Continental T-6 engine) added inherent design flaws to the equation: Its lack of side ventilation louvers on the engine cowl worsened the overheating problems.

In urban areas where water and other amenities were plentiful, these technical matters rarely aroused concern. However, when long-distance travel dictated the navigation of unpopulated regions of the Southwest—especially over the Sitgreaves Pass in Arizona—thoughts were quickly dominated by desolate desert stereotypes. So-called "last chance" gas stations didn't waste time capitalizing on the worries: posted warnings implored motorists to fill up with fuel and water. Billboards adorned with skull and crossbones reinforced the message, conjuring images of stranded travelers perishing of thirst.

To ease their panic, motorists relied on portable "water bags" to carry along extra liquid. Originally intended to transport drink-

The canvas water bag was at one time a familiar sight along the distant miles of Highway 66. To complete the desert crossings in Arizona, motorists relied on a portable container to hold their drinking (and sometimes radiator) water. Slung over the hood of a speeding car or hung outside a window, evaporation cooled the contents of the bag making it more palatable to drink. *Author*

ing water for human consumption, these soft containers were universally adopted by cross-country drivers as insurance policies for radiator boil-over. During the heyday of America's maternal two-lane, the practice of topping off one's bag before a journey heightened to near religious fervor. It was a ritual repeated along the entire length of the 2,400 mile strip, rivaled only by gas tanks being filled with motor fuel!

While design of the bags varied, the standard models were specially woven from Scotch Flax or "genuine imported linen." For less than a one-dollar bill, the conscientious vehicle owner could purchase a sack from well-stocked service stations, auto supply houses, and general stores. Rectangular in configuration, the typical canvas container featured heavy border stitching and a removable cap—secured from loss by string or chain. Some sported a flat, wooden carrying handle with hand-hold. To facilitate easy hanging on the exterior of the vehicle, most came with a heavy-duty rope looped through eyelets.

On the exterior, bold graphics distinguished the competitors: the well-known "Safari" brand featured a roaring lion, "Hirsch Weis" a vaulting buck, and "Water Boy" a feathered Indian. W.A. Plummer's classic pick and shovel design flaunted the worrisome bromide, "Desert Water Bag." Even the Pep Boys got in on the action! Speeding across the desert in a convertible, the grinning caricatures of Manny, Moe, and Jack appeared fearless as they hurtled across the no-man's land of sagebrush and saguaro.

It was an appropriate image, since forward motion is what actually made the bags work. After filling with water, they began to perspire with moisture as liquid leached through the special strands of cloth. When draped outside of a window, slung over the hood ornament, or hung on the side-mounted spare, air rushing over their exterior created an effect likened to "wind chill." The intense evaporation caused contents inside the pouch to cool. So, instead of heating up to the outside ambient air temperature, water remained "cool and palatable."

Despite the clever principles involved, the chilling novelty of the desert water bag eventually faded. For the thirsty, the insulated ice-chest and vacuum flask Thermos became standard equipment for mobile dining. Automotive technologies advanced as well, resulting in the introduction of improved formulations for artificial coolant. Chemically protected in conditions hot or cold, engines evolved into efficient and powerful machines—virtually free from the specter of thermal breakdown.

By the 1950s, the requirement to tote a dripping udder of extra water east and west along Route 66 was all but eliminated. The venerable water purse was tossed into the trunk, discarded, and gladly forgotten. It was—and always would be—a reminder of the days when motoring across America required a pioneering spirit, a full gas tank, and a bulging desert water bag.

The Elmer Thomas family of migrants stopped in the Oklahoma town of Muskogee for some water in 1939. To refill the reservoir, the combination hood ornament and radiator cap was removed (note the elaborate crest he is holding) and the water poured in. Specialized antifreeze was the least of Mr. Thomas's worries. Russell Lee photo, 1939. *Library of Congress*

Wichita, Kansas, was the home for Valentine Diners, a post-WWII manufacturer that made prefabricated dining units for the roadside trade. A variety of aluminum models were offered, all numbered and leased to operators eager to make a fast buck. While most diners are typically located in New England, the Valentine units are found all across the country, and of course, various spots on Route 66. The Birthplace Diner was located on the site of Winslow's first dwelling and at one time had a miniature stork planted on top of it (to honor its historic location). Thelma Holloway was the first to manage this minuscule lunch counter. Most recently, it changed to Leon Dodd's One Spot Grill. *Jerry McClanahan ©1995*

AT THE CROSSROADS
OF U. S. HIGHWAYS
66 AND 77

GARLAND'S
DRIVE-IN
RESTAURANT

OKLAHOMA'S
FINEST

22nd and Broadway

OKLAHOMA CITY

Phone 5-8811

SEA FOOD   BARBECUE   CURB SERVICE

22ND STREET

At the crossroads of Highways 66 and 77 in Oklahoma City, Oklahoma, Garland's Drive-In took its rooftop sign to the limit. Originally incorporated into building architecture to circumvent local sign regulations, the idea of a tall, central spire bedecked with neon lettering was a concept embraced by curb servers all across the country. *Preziosi Postcards*

During the 1930s, California Route 66 was thick with orange juice stands. Everybody it seemed was getting into the orange juice business, eager to sell their crop of squeezed citrus to the carloads of arrivees coming in on the great diagonal highway. Many larger restaurants and dining chains got their start in this manner, including a small refreshment stand run by Richard and Maurice McDonald, founders of the now ubiquitous McDonald's chain of hamburger eateries. Route 66, Rialto, California. *Author*

The ribbons of Route 66 roadway like the one found near Fenner, California, are the lengths of vintage highway that often stimulate the appetite. During miles and miles of long-distance driving, evidence of civilization is often sparse—driving the motorist's imagination to visions of full-service gasoline stations offering ice water, drive-in restaurants delivering cold drinks, and wayside cafes serving up freshly grilled cheeseburgers. *D. Jeanene Tiner ©1995*

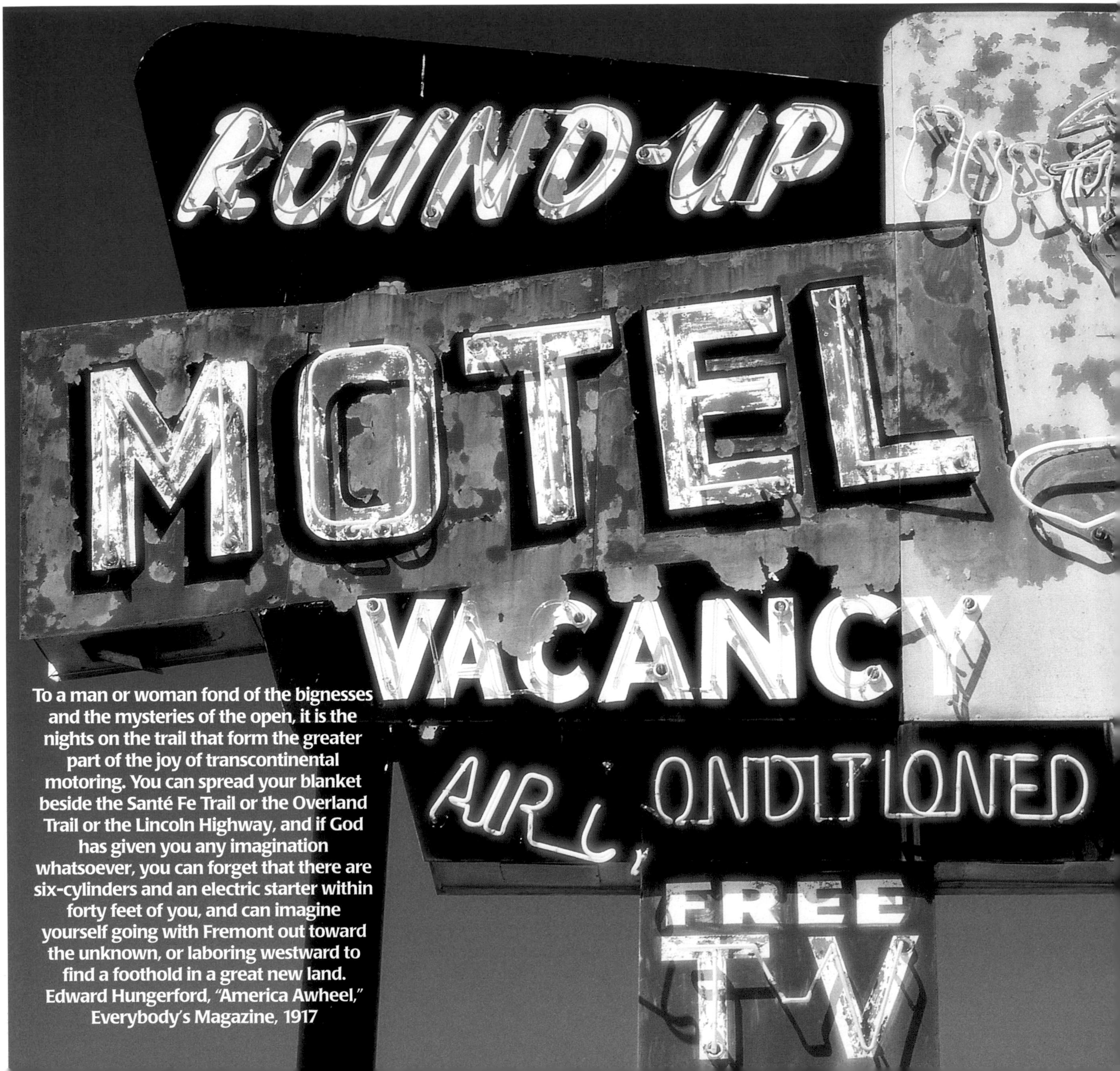

chapter four

ROUND-UP

MOTEL

VACANCY

AIR CONDITIONED

FREE TV

To a man or woman fond of the bignesses and the mysteries of the open, it is the nights on the trail that form the greater part of the joy of transcontinental motoring. You can spread your blanket beside the Santé Fe Trail or the Overland Trail or the Lincoln Highway, and if God has given you any imagination whatsoever, you can forget that there are six-cylinders and an electric starter within forty feet of you, and can imagine yourself going with Fremont out toward the unknown, or laboring westward to find a foothold in a great new land.
Edward Hungerford, "America Awheel," Everybody's Magazine, 1917

Motor Hotels:
America's Home on the Road

Regarding convenience and comfort, the slow-moving tortoise has an obvious advantage over the speeding motorist! When a day's travel comes to a close, he has no worries over where he might sleep. He simply picks out a serene spot, withdraws his appendages, retracts his head, and remains still until rested. Inside his shell he is safe, warm, and protected. When circumstances call for relocation to a new environment, his self-contained, portable accommodations move right along with him. It's an idea that has been admired by the automobile owner since the debut of the gas-powered engine and a concept that has been experimented with since the dirt road days of Route 66.

Of all the collectibles pertaining to Route 66, the common matchbook remains one of the easiest artifacts to acquire. In the days before smoking was considered a nuisance, hotels, motels, and other roadside businesses distributed these hand-held gems to advertise their accommodations. *Courtesy Chuck Sturm*

left
Along the shoulder of the old road, Western themes have always dominated motel sign graphics. In Oklahoma, Texas, New Mexico, and Arizona, the predominant subjects were, and continue to be, rough-riding cowboys, colorful Indians, Longhorn cattle, and the ubiquitous Saguaro cactus. It's all part of the illusion designed to make travelers feel as if they have reached the destination imagined in their mind's eye. Claremore, Oklahoma. *Author*

121

The Boots Motel is prime example of the architectural stylings popularized during the 1930s and 1940s. With its rounded corners, distinctive "speed lines," and pastel accents, it's one of the roadside resources of Route 66 that should not be missed. Carthage, Missouri. *Shellee Graham © 1995*

Unfortunately, the pioneering motor vehicle operator of the early 1900s didn't have such an easy go of it. Back then, a long-distance journey across the expanse of America was described best by the etymology of the word "travel." Originally, this innocuous expression was derived from the French *travail*, meaning work and trouble. Further iteration cites the Latin *trepalium*, a three-staked instrument of torture! It's an apt description, since the pitfalls and problems encountered by the automotive enthusiast at the turn of the century were numerous. Spending the nights along the trail meant a reliance upon one's own resources.

In that regard, automobilists so inclined to risk life and limb simply to prove that they could drive a motor coach all the way across America and "dip their wheels in the Pacific" found it prudent to stock up on equipment germane to the explorer. Tents, kerosene lanterns, portable cooking equipment, bedrolls, hunting gear—and a myriad of other camping paraphernalia—became required baggage for would-be adventurers hooked on four-wheeled overland transportation.

On occasion, car travelers could take advantage of the hotel facilities offered in some of the larger cities. But for numerous reasons, these were avoided by intrepid explorers addicted to the smell of gasoline and burning motor oil. With money reserved for more important incidentals such as tire patches, extraction from mud holes, or mechanical repair, paying for the

Although closed and abandoned, the Rest Haven Motel still boasts a fetching roadside sign. While much of the neon is broken and the electricity disconnected, it continues to attract the gaze of all those in search of the past. Afton, Oklahoma. *Author*

privilege to recline on a lumpy mattress and have a tip-hungry bellman carry one's baggage was the last thing any self-respecting adventurer wanted to do.

At the same time, there were obvious issues of appearance to consider. Entering an establishment with grease-splattered driving goggles, soiled gauntlets, and a duster thick with road dirt was often viewed with great trepidation by both the desk clerks and hotel management. At the boarding houses that catered to a less affluent class, the reverse was true: Those arriving in the motorcars were the ones uncomfortable with the surroundings and social strata of the clientele.

As a result, the open spaces that bordered the public highways and byways became attractive venues for travelers to set up temporary sleeping accommodations. When tired eyes called for rest, one simply decelerated, turned the steering wheel right or left, and coasted into the nearest clearing. Outdoors, natural amenities provided roving travelers with free facilities, unencumbered by monetary and social constraints often imposed by the urban hotel.

In the "great outdoors," wood for campfires was readily accessible, water could be carried from streams, and personal facilities were abundant. When answering the call of nature, one sought refuge behind a substantial tree and took care of business. In the natural environment of the undeveloped roadside, there were no monitors, no rules. Best of all, there was always plenty of free parking!

At first, landowners who found themselves host to visitors tolerated the infrequent forays onto their property and sometimes even offered the hand of hospitality. The friendliness proved short-lived, however, and even turned to loathing as more and more motorists ventured past city limits in search of scenery and solitude. When Henry Ford introduced the affordable Model T in 1908, the days of unbridled activities along the roadside were destined to end. Within two short years, there were 468,500 registered motor vehicles plying the roadways with a substantial number placing undue demands on rural real estate.

To quell the unsupervised actions of overnight freeloaders, farmers and landowners with property bisected by highways began to adopt a stricter attitude *continued on page 128*

In the beginning, America's auto camps offered little luxury. In most cases, visitors arriving by automobile had to fend for themselves when it came to water and toilet facilities. Fortunately, the situation began to improve by the 1940s with the advent of "sanitary facilities." Slowly but surely, the American outhouse was fading into oblivion. Southern California, Russell Lee photo, 1940. *Library of Congress*

Frank Redford's Wigwam Village Motels

*"Occasionally, customers got more than their money's worth when Native American dancers
imported from Oklahoma demonstrated the lost art of rainmaking."*

During the 1950s, "cowboys and Indians" was a favorite game for children. Back then, the airwaves were populated by characters like Buffalo Bob Smith, Hopalong Cassidy, The Lone Ranger and Tonto. A craze for the West permeated American popular culture and businesses along 66 did all they could to fuel the frenzy. Motel showman Frank Redford led the pack.

It all started in the early 1930s with a cone-shaped ice cream stand in Long Beach, California. Inspired by the design, Redford built a filling station and cafe in Horse Cave, Kentucky. When it opened in 1933, the tourists visiting nearby Mammoth Cave could hardly believe their eyes: Indian teepees were sprouting along Highway 31E! The "main office" was a 60-foot tall construction of wood and stucco, enhanced by a matching pair of "wigwam" rest rooms.

After repeated requests from customers for overnight cabins, Redford added six "sleeping rooms" in 1935. A year later, he patented the exterior design of the teepees and proceeded to field inquiries from entrepreneurs eager to open their own roadside camp. Over the next 15 years, the Wigwam Villages grew into a modest motel chain with seven sites in six states. Two of the most celebrated reservations made their home along the Will Rogers Highway.

Appropriately, Wigwam Village number six occupied a lot on Hopi Drive in Holbrook, Arizona. As Route 66 rose in prominence, it became a premier tourist attraction for motorists traveling through "the heart of Indian country." When number seven was completed in 1947, the Foothill Boulevard section through San Bernardino, California, gained new status on the road maps. Curious carloads came to take snapshots, stay overnight, or just plain look. Both locations became recognized landmarks—part and parcel of getting one's kicks along Route 66.

For the unjaded motorist on holiday, the Indian motif had unquestionable allure. And why not? Near the road, a teepee-shaped sign provided a modern version of the smoke signal in neon, imploring all those who passed to "Eat and Sleep in a Wigwam!" Auto excursionists were enchanted by the idea and eagerly checked-in to experience the wonders. Upon their departure, teepee-shaped menus and plaster replicas were purchased as treasured souvenirs.

Redford was more than willing to feed the fantasies, at one point hiring a trio of young Indian lads as helpers. Occasionally, customers got more than their money's worth when Native American dancers imported from Oklahoma demonstrated the lost art of rainmaking.

Fortunately, the teepees were impervious to the elements and well insulated for the "peace and quiet" of overnight patrons. The internal framework consisted of wood timbers arranged to form a multi-sided cone then covered in tar paper. Stucco was plastered on to fashion the faux "cowhide" skin, artfully sculpted at each entryway to give the appearance of a rolled back flap. Similarly, the four lodgepoles that projected up through the tip were for visual effect only.

Outside, the exterior paint scheme was decidedly subdued, enhancing the roadside illusion. The majority of the teepee surface was finished with a coat of bright white paint. At the vertex of each hut, a contrasting splash of red was edged with a sublime border of zigzag. A similar course of colorful rickrack encircled the middle circumference of each cabin, leading the eye to an ornamental line surrounding the unit's diamond-shaped window.

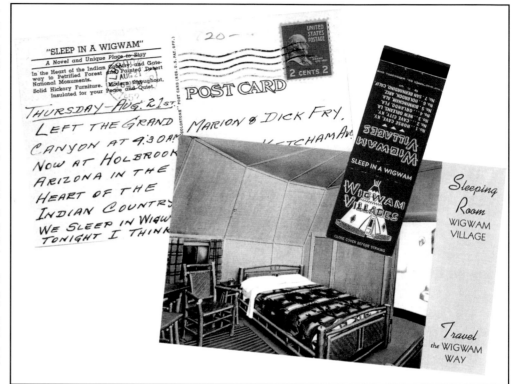

One of the most memorable attributes of the Wigwam Villages were their interiors. Proprietor Frank Redford furnished the cabins with authentic Navajo and Apache rugs and blankets. A suite of real hickory furniture—with the bark still in place—completed the rustic atmosphere. Holbrook, Arizona.
Courtesy Chuck Sturm

Inside, all of the modern conveniences were available. Full bathroom facilities with a shower, sink, and toilet pleased even the most discerning tribe. While a fire would have been stoked in a real wigwam, heating was provided by a thermostatically controlled steam radiator. Electrical outlets delivered power for Mom's portable iron and Dad's Zenith Trans-Oceanic radio.

In the decor department, the teepee interiors were carefully orchestrated to indulge the notions of what a "real" western lodge should look like. A suite of rustic furniture included a bed, night stand, and chair—all fashioned from natural hickory wood with the bark still in place. Redford supplied the rooms with authentic Apache Indian blankets, Navajo rugs, teepee-shaped table lamps, and wigwam ashtrays. Of course, the wall-to-wall paneling was knotty-pine!

With that accomplished, Redford's Wigwam Villages satisfied two of the traveler's most important needs: lodging and adventure. For a single fare, the typical family was allowed to stay in a comfy motel room and experience the delights of an authentic roadside attraction. Along the marvelous miles of old Route 66, no amount of wampum could buy a better deal.

Partners Frank Redford and his wife, Vetra, operated Kentucky's Wigwam Village Motel with the help of Redford's mother, Sally Ann. Through a combination of unusual architecture, teamwork, and high moral standards, they made the Wigwam Villages into the most-recognized icons of Highway 66. *Keith A. Sculle Collection*

When compared to common building methods, construction of the teepee sleeping units was unconventional. At first, they were made with a steel framework covered by lath and plaster. After a number of chronic problems surfaced with that design, the method was modified to make the buildings more like boat hulls. Applied to each steel cabin frame was a layer of wood, a layer of felt, and a covering of canvas. Finally, a generous amount of linseed oil was applied to shrink the structures until they were finally covered with stucco and painted. Wigwam Village No. 5, Birmingham, Alabama, 1940s. *Keith A. Sculle Collection*

The Wigwam Village (located on Hopi Drive in Holbrook, Arizona) is one of the last pristine examples of the teepee motel chain begun by Frank Redford after World War II. Today, all those in search of the old road—and the landmarks that made it what it was—may still spend the night there. Although the modern motel chains are nice, there's still nothing that can beat the fun of "sleeping in a wigwam." *Shellee Graham ©1995*

ENJOY REAL WESTERN HOSPITALITY

SILVER SPUR MOTEL

EAST AMARILLO, TEXAS — ON U. S. HIGHWAYS 60 & 66

1C-H656

Americans vacationing by car have always been enamored with the concept of the West, and Route 66 motels fueled the fantasy with a variety of cowboy themes. But whether it was the Silver Spur, the Longhorn, Golden Saddle, Wagon Wheel, or the Branding Iron, it really didn't matter. All served up a heaping helping of the "real western hospitality" so craved by the public. East Amarillo, Texas. *Preziosi Postcards*

right
While Bailey's Motel was basically a simple, contiguous structure under one roof, it really painted a romantic image for itself with its lasso-roping postcard. In the real world, the rooms featured pretty much the same type of furniture and bathroom fixtures found at a majority of the motels in town, although "Panelray Heat" was touted as one of the unique amenities. What was it? Simply a vertical gas burner set into the wall and individually controlled by the room's occupant. It was the next best thing to a real campfire on the open range. Amarillo, Texas. *Preziosi Postcards*

continued from page 125

toward the ever-increasing swarms of motorized locusts descending on their land. And who could blame them? The thoughtless crowds arriving by car were making a mess of the countryside, helping themselves to shrubs, trampling fields, and picking orchards clean. Cows were milked dry without permission and crops harvested for a quick roadside snack. In one dramatic incident, a crowd of car campers accidentally set fire to a landowner's woods while another bunch tore off entire branches from the trees.

By 1925, the unbridled activities had reached the breaking point, and a number of national magazines published scathing articles critical of the

AILEY'S MOTEL

TH AVE. — PHONE 2-0423 — AMARILLO, TEXAS

The rustic log cabin was a popular structure for independent motel operators in the Missouri Ozarks. They were a common sight along Route 66 during the 1940s and 1950s. John's "Modern" Cabins have stood the test of time, and although completely abandoned, they have become a much-admired and visited landmark along the old road south of Rolla, Missouri. Bypassed by new asphalt, the decaying shells may still be visited along a dead end stretch of Route 66 frontage. *Dan Harlow ©1995*

phenomenon. One fed-up farmer summed up the problem when he explained how motorists "would turn into the meadow without saying so much as by your leave; pitch their tent, collect firewood, cook supper, and then start hell-raising as if the whole place had been made over to them by deed!" A change was coming.

Part of the new relationship with automobile owners was to prohibit their entry onto private property. Barbed wire was strung along the shoulder, joined by fencing and other barriers to keep the so-called "hurrah boys" from spoiling areas adjacent to the public corridors. "No Trespassing" and "Keep Out" signs became a part of the scenery. To emphasize their position, a few farmers kept watch with their shotguns close at hand. To deter would-be visitors from setting up overnight encampments, a vicious-looking dog secured by what appeared to be a weak chain proved to be one of the most effective strategies. Like it or not, the uninhibited lifestyle of the motoring camper was drawing to a close.

At the same time, businessmen in towns along Highway 66 and other routes realized that this unorganized rabble of "game, fish, and flower hogs" could be readily tapped as a substantial source of income. The consensus was that if the throngs of sputtering

Some trailer courts and auto camps furnished laundry facilities to their boarders. Because there was an additional charge levied to use electric washing machines, an area was reserved for the manual agitation and rinsing of clothes. Of course, there were certain rules and protocol to follow to ensure that the equipment was clean and in good order for the next customer. Southern California, Russell Lee photo, 1940. *Library of Congress*

automobiles could be influenced to set up their camps in organized parks near the city limits, all the businesses lining Main Street and other urban areas would be patronized for groceries, clothing goods, automotive supplies, and other services.

To test the theory, many towns erected municipal camps that offered free space where motorists could

left
The 66 Motel is one of Tulsa's surviving motor courts. Found at the outskirts of town on a part of the old road alignment that cuts through an industrial area, it continues to house travelers exploring the back roads. Noma Undernehr is the current owner of this forgotten treasure on the edge. *Author*

pitch a tent, roll out a bedroll, or slumber in their rumble seat. Along with complimentary campsites, the municipal operations featured all the basic conveniences so sorely lacking along the nation's highways. Public privies were installed for personal hygiene and there was even running water available for washing clothes and cooking. At some of the better camps, one could find playgrounds for the children, bathing facilities,

and electrical hookups. At long last, America's hoards of auto-campers had a cheap, easy-to-access oasis at their disposal. Along Highway 66 and other roads like it, the municipal camps surged in popularity.

Like the cities, the manufacturers of travel gadgets saw a great potential for sales and soon introduced a host of products geared to the car club. One of the most popular contrivances was the "auto-

Massage of the Magic Fingers Mattress

"Sampling the subtle waves of relaxation emanating from his reconfigured recliner, he coined the phrase 'Magic Fingers' and set upon the task of marketing it to the masses."

During the twilight of the 1950s, the Englander Company manufactured a commercial mattress with a mechanical vibrator at its core. One of its top salesmen, John Houghtaling (pronounced hotel-ing), peddled the unit to customers in the lodging industry. When a number of clients complained that the massagers were burning out, he took it upon himself to find out why.

For almost two years, he conducted a relentless campaign of under-bed research. Mattresses were dissected, bedsprings analyzed, and motors monitored. After disassembling the mysterious motion transducer and studying its intricate workings, he discovered that "there wasn't much to it." Inside, what was initially perceived as a mechanized marvel consisted of nothing more than a simple electric motor with a small counterweight attached to its driveshaft.

Houghtaling began to tinker on his own and soon devised a much more reliable version. It was small, powerful, and a snap to replace. Best of all, his visionary design had a specific advantage over the existing competition: it could easily be mated with any mattress. Now, anyone handy with a screwdriver could install one of these new massagers—right to the inside of a bed's box spring! A quad arrangement of special, grooved mounting posts made easy work of attaching the vibro-module between the cushioning coils. The inventive Houghtaling wisely patented his unique design approach.

Sampling the subtle waves of relaxation emanating from his reconfigured recliner, he coined the phrase "Magic Fingers" and set upon the task of marketing it to the masses. Sales representatives from across the country were recruited in a loose franchise arrangement. For an investment of $2,500, would-be dealers received 80 of the vibrator units, three days of training, and audio-visual materials. After that, it was the dealer's responsibility to locate potential customers, handle installation, facilitate repairs, and finally, collect the sacks of coins accumulated at the end of each month.

A compact control head (attached by wire) held the loot and activated the magical oscillations. Bolted down securely (in later years) to the night stand, it served as both a pay receptacle and housing for the timer. When sleepy overnighters dropped one quarter into the coin meter, it tripped a mechanism—allowing 15 minutes of operation. The setup worked without a hitch for a number of years until basic honesty went the way of the dodo. Suddenly, anyone and everyone (including some motel employees) began breaking into the coin meters to help themselves to the proceeds!

For the hapless distributor, the resulting losses could be quite substantial. During the heyday of Magic Fingers mania, over 250,000 units were buzzing along at both the independent and major chain accommodations nationwide. With an average of eight quarters brought in by each unit during the time span of one month, an entrepreneur maintaining a few hundred vibrators could pull in a considerable chunk of change. Since Houghtaling didn't demand royalties, top salesmen could make a good living.

By the 1970s, an aggressive attempt was made to thwart the pilferage by employing magnetic stripe technology.

Room renters received a card from the desk clerk during check-in that could be credited with incremental amounts of time. Back in the privacy of their rooms, a modified control head read the debit card and activated the Magic Fingers. Unfortunately, costs to continually upgrade the system to reflect the latest technology were prohibitive. Card readers that were initially "high-tech" were quickly rendered obsolete by the fast pace of progress.

Eventually, coin theft became such a problem that Houghtaling couldn't sell distributorships with a clear conscience. Somebody would set up business and effectively go broke in just a few months.

During the halcyon days of roadside lodging, the progressive proprietors of hotels, motels, and tourist courts like the Blue Swallow learned of the Magic Fingers unit in industry publications like *Tourist Court Journal*. Along with the coin-operated radio and the soda machine, it was perceived by some as a cost-effective way to maximize profits from overnight patrons. With its ease of installation and affordability, Magic Fingers quickly joined "refrigerated air" and "a television in every room" as yet another popular amenity. Tucumcari, New Mexico. *Jerry McClanahan ©1995*

But the Magic Fingers wasn't licked yet: In the early 1980s, the General Stamping and Manufacturing Company of Hialeah, Florida, acquired rights to the gizmo and began marketing it to residential customers. While demand from the motel industry waned, seniors remembered the therapeutic gadgets from their cross-country journeys on Route 66 and eagerly purchased them for home use—albeit, without the coin meters.

Today, fully functional models of the venerable Magic Fingers mattress can still be discovered—and enjoyed—at a smattering of tourist courts, cabins, and no-tell motels along the retired recesses of Highway 66. Along with "refrigerated air" and "a television in every room," Houghtaling's shimmying shaker has found a place of permanence in the pop culture of the American road. Anybody got change for a buck?

DIAGRAM OF VIBRATOR INSTALLED IN BOX SPRINGS

During the days before extensive thought was put into auto interiors, motoring vast distances along Route 66 could be quite grueling. After all, spartan bench seats offered little support for the lower lumbar region. Without cruise-control, the accelerator foot tired quickly. The absence of power steering brought on tired shoulders and wrist cramps. Lacking today's ergonomics, cars could be rolling torture chambers. Fortunately, America's burgeoning motel industry came to the rescue by equipping rentals with therapeutic aids. During the 1960s, travelers obsessed with arriving in "Tucumcari Tonight" were rewarded with a massage therapist in every room! How could they do it? Simple: Every bed was equipped with a shimmying shaker. For only 25 cents, a bed vibrator soothed spines, relaxed muscles, and calmed travelers to a restful slumber. *Courtesy General Stamping & Mfg. Co.*

During the 1940s, the Hotel Franciscan was one of the highlights of staying overnight in Albuquerque, New Mexico. An initial glance suggests another incarnation of the adobe Pueblo, but further examination reveals distinct Art-Deco overtones as well as hints of the International style. As part of the concept, roof timbers have become idealized drainpipes and windows stylized portals. Note the unique sign on the gun store to the left of the building. John Collier photo, 1943. *Library of Congress*

Along the Santa Fe Trail in Missouri, travelers of the early teens had only two choices when it came to lodging: sleep in established hotels in the cities along the way, or make a camp out in the open wilderness. Horseless carriage owners were sometimes frowned upon because of their disheveled appearance, hence the wide open spaces were often chosen to avoid scrutiny. Missouri, A.L. Westgard photo, circa 1912. *National Archives*

tent," a collapsible camping device that mounted right onto the running board of an automobile. When time came to set up camp, it was unfolded by the enthusiast into a full-sized shelter—complete with a cot for sleeping, support springs, and a built-in headrest (the running board). For the growing ranks of car owners anxious to experience the adventures of auto-camping, it was the perfect vacation accessory for the open road.

Warner's Autotrailer "Prairie Schooner" took the tent idea to the next level with a collapsible sleeping unit that attached to

DEDICATED TO WILL ROGERS. THE WORLD'S GREATEST HUMORIST, CLAREMORE, OKLA., U. S. A.

the rear bumper. A distant cousin to the "pop-up" trailers that would appear decades later, it sported two wheels attached to a compact trailer compartment. Inside the box, a rather complex arrangement of poles and canvas were stored until it was time to set up camp. Once assembled, the Auto-trailer was the envy of all the auto-

campers—that is—until time came to put it all back in the box again. For those who experienced difficulty in folding a service station roadmap, breaking down this unit and fitting it back in the rolling compart-ment was a daunting task. Onlookers gained a new admiration for the simplicity of a pup tent.

The Hotel Will Rogers was dedicated on February 7, 1930. After the ceremony, Rogers himself said, "I was more proud to see my name in electric lights in my old home town on an institution built for service to the public, than I ever was on the biggest theater on Broadway." Since the hotel made a commitment to offering "That Eastern Atmosphere, Western Welcome, and Southern Hospitality," Rogers' statement was more than mere hyperbole. Claremore, Oklahoma. *Courtesy Chuck Sturm*

135

The Nelson Dream Village was an annex to the famous Nelson Tavern. On the grounds, visitors could thrill to the Musical Fountain and drive right up to rooms that featured a free garage. The individual "Guest Houses" were built to resemble storybook cottages and allowed renters to lose themselves in a distinct roadside "world." While such an establishment might be considered hokey if judged by today's standards, it was an appropriate format for an age that lacked Disneyworld, Six Flags, and the Universal Studios Tour. Lebanon, Missouri. *Preziosi Postcards*

Still, the availability of new camping equipment wasn't the only force that contributed to the municipal camp's success. The profusion of new vehicles taking to the highways was a more likely cause. Statistics released in 1924 by the Automobile Association of America revealed that well over 16 million motor vehicles were in operation nationwide. It was estimated that each motorcar was driven an average of 5,000 miles every year with 10 percent of the travel time

devoted to what the pundits referred to as the "gypsy pilgrimage."

As patronage of the municipal camps swelled, a whole new set of problems developed. First and foremost were concerns about the ability to overnight at a camp for free. While the complimentary arrangement was a desirable incentive for the typical traveler, it attracted a fair number of "undesirables." Unemployed drifters, con-artists, ex-convicts, door-to-door salesmen, and other shifty characters arranged semi-

Reed's Cabins were some of the coziest on the Missouri side of the Mississippi. Sure, they weren't anything fancy, but at least they provided a cheap place to stay for a family heading west. Today, simple overnight courts like Reed's are getting harder to come by. A sparse few remain as forgotten footnotes to the golden age of Highway 66. Carthage, Missouri. *Courtesy Chuck Sturm*

During the mid-1920s to late 1930s, the average conveniences along Route 66 were quite modest. Motel accommodations were simple, unadorned, and utilitarian in nature. After all, people traveling away from home by automobile were happy enough just to get a roof over their heads. It seems curious that in those days, society got along just fine without all the swimming pools, fitness centers, and fax machines so cherished by today's highway adventurers. Vinita, Oklahoma. *Courtesy Chuck Sturm*

permanent housing simply by driving up with an old clunker and setting up housekeeping on the running boards. Their freeloading was causing both a monetary and social strain.

As the problem worsened, legitimate customers who had funds to buy fuel from the camp-run gas station or foodstuffs from the adjoining grocery store grew concerned over the declining ambiance. As news of the conditions spread throughout the regions of Route 66, the idea of a "free" motor camp took on a decidedly negative connotation.

In an effort to rehabilitate the public's perception of their facilities, many camp outfits decided that it would be best to charge a nominal fee to motoring campers. That way, the increasing mob of out-of-gas malingerers and motor-hobos would be

½ Mi. South of Vinita, Oklahoma on U.S. 66 - 69 - 60

137

Signs—especially brightly lit neon signs with loud colors—are what once attracted customers to the highway motor courts. Out on the road, these glaring messages mounted high atop a pole were often the first thing seen amid the cacophony of billboards and roadside advertising. During the 1950s, a neon clock mounted above the front entryway was standard. Tulsa, Oklahoma. *Author*

forced to relocate when their money was depleted. The concept worked, allowing the proprietors of the municipal camps to effectively relocate the shiftless overnighter.

Unfortunately, the implementation of this pay-as-you-stay policy came too late. The damage was already done and it seemed that no amount of public relations could polish the tarnished image of the organized roadside camp. For all intents and purposes,

The Pueblo Bonito Motel was one of Albuquerque's finest accommodations. Located on Highway 66 (2424 West Central Avenue), it featured the adobe Pueblo style of architecture so admired in the Southwest. Large, three- and two-bedroom apartments with kitchenettes were available, each room featuring air-conditioning, an automatic floor furnace, tile bath, custom-built Franciscan furniture, and an enclosed heated garage. During WWII, defense workers used the facilities as temporary housing. Albuquerque, New Mexico, John Collier photo, 1943. *Library of Congress*

Sign Language Neon of the Motel Marquee

"Ever eager to please, the proprietors of hotels and motels incorporated a variety of regional stereotypes into their signage."

*F*orty years ago, nothing could compare to the razzle dazzle of lights witnessed along roadside 66. As twilight descended upon the two-lane, the illuminated signs of motor courts, motels, and tourist cabins assumed dominance over the night. In a kaleidoscope of color, miles of neon flickered to life with a new language—an iconic code intended solely for automotive occupants.

Leading the dialogue in this lexicon of light was the unpretentious indicator of availability: the "vacancy" sign. If accommodations were booked solid, the dimmed portion of this signal was illuminated. From the highway, one could tell at a glance whether or not a motel had empty rooms. For the motorist, it was the one key element of an advertising billboard that determined whether or not to read on.

At the next level, tourist court terminology required a bit more scrutiny. While the ice blue characters of "air conditioning" teased the senses with frosty twists of neon, a degree of caution was called for before one actually signed a guest register. In the formative years preceding the perfection of personal indoor comfort, this deceptive catch-phrase routinely referred to an ordinary heating system or centralized fan!

Likewise, the words "air-cooled" couldn't be relied upon to provide substantial heat relief. The reality of this slogan was more suggestion than actual fact. In layman's terms, it described the possibilities of a process known as evaporative cooling—a crude arrangement that relied on a water-breathing leviathan, known affectionately (to traveling salesmen and residents of Arizona) as the "swamp cooler." The only sign language that guaranteed a chilled breeze was "air-cooled by refrigeration."

With matters of comfort addressed, the motoring crowd looked to the motel sign for entertainment clues. For some, the ability to catch the latest episode of "I Love Lucy" was just as important as indoor climate. But simply qualifying a sign for the word "television" wasn't always enough. By the time the would-be watcher realized the screen was coin-operated, it was too late. "Free T.V." was the correct combo to look for if one desired unlimited tube time.

For vacationers unconcerned with the pratfalls of the Ricardo family or the humidity of their cabin, a sign that stirred the imagination was often reason enough to pull over. Ever eager to please, the proprietors of hotels and motels incorporated a variety of regional stereotypes into their signage. Recurring themes included past presidents, animals, the westward movement, Indians, and of course, cowboys.

Not surprisingly, the western mystique was the most popular theme along Route 66, even in the Midwest. Consider the rustic Wagon Wheel Motel in the village of Cuba, Missouri: with an uncluttered arrangement of bow-legged letters and a wooden-spoke wheel, it rustled up childhood fantasies filled with prairie schooners and cattle drives. Once upon a time along the Will Rogers Highway, just the idea of the "West" was enough to sell motel rooms.

As the real gateway to the West was breached in Oklahoma and then Texas, the down-home dialect of the motel signs turned to twang. Suddenly, idealized depictions of cowboys riding the range on horseback whooped it up in blazing

A view looking west down old Route 66 in Holbrook, Arizona. As in many of the tourist towns found along the great diagonal highway, Holbrook's motel row is a neon dream of the urban boulevard. *Jerry McClanahan ©1995*

color. Wild stallions reared, snorted, and galloped in curves of animated neon. The lasso—primary tool for the cowpoke—became an integral part of a sign's message. In most cases, it twirled out from the roper's hand to spell out a variety of catchy come-ons in golden strokes of yellow light. It was one wild ride!

Of course, Native Americans received an equal amount of sign coverage, minus the buckaroos. The proud profile of a generic Chief wearing a feathered headdress became the most common design, a tomahawk-toting brave running close second. Some court-tels tried to model their signposts after totem poles or Hopi Kachinas, but most remained true to the fanciful perceptions born of the tourist's vivid imagination. For the drowsy driver exploring 66, the visual vocabulary of the American motel marquee made up one convincing sales pitch. *They* were the reason we chose to exit the road—because when it came right down to it, rented bed and bathrooms were almost identical. The real differences were burning brightly up on those amazing billboards of light, electrified representations of what ideal overnight accommodations could be, should be and not what they really were.

The Cotton Boll motel probably saw more travelers heading to western vacations than it did cotton pickers. Consisting of a small L-shaped motel without garages, it remains as a prime example of the simple motel structure with connected sleeping units. As of the mid-1990s, the "vacancy" sign was still lit. East of Elk City in Canute, Oklahoma, 1983. *Jerry McClanahan ©1995*

the idea of parking bumper-to-bumper with perfect strangers in a roadside auto-camp had lost most of its appeal. The motorized vacationer was growing more sophisticated.

With the premise of paying for a place to spend the night established, the way was cleared for a new type of accommodation that would solve many of the privacy issues of the public camps: the rented cabin. As municipal concerns were scrambling to refine their services, a handful of trendsetters along America's Main Street anticipated the trend toward fully enclosed sleeping quarters and began constructing modest bungalows on property adjoining the highway.

While the pioneering units were Spartan affairs that offered no more than four walls and a floor, they ushered in an era of

The snorting Palomino Motel sign is convincing evidence that the American cowboy and his trusty steed were (and in some cases still are) staple images of Highway 66 advertising. Throughout the western states along the route, neon tubing has routinely assumed the shape of cattlemen, Longhorn steer, cowboy boots, and a variety of related archetypes. Unlike today's unattractive signboards with their internal lighting and vacuum-formed plastic, the illuminated salesmen of yesterday's road possessed a charm all their own. Tucumcari, New Mexico. *Jerry McClanahan ©1995*

141

66 Courts in Groom, Texas, was the typical small town motel with a house converted to an office flanked by a row of stucco sleeping units for overnighters. Although the house is now history, the stucco units are still standing, along with the roadside sign. Beneath, a rusted, derelict Edsel riddled with bullet holes provides an engaging photo-opportunity for all those passing through. *Jim Ross ©1995*

privacy previously unknown by auto-campers. After a long day's drive , both pilot and passenger could relax in their skivvies without worry. There were no limitations to the freedoms that might be enjoyed behind closed cabin doors.

The advantages were numerous. By renting a cabin, tourists could travel lighter. No longer was there any need to carry all the equipment required of a safari when embarking on a motor journey. Since cabins provided a watertight roof, insulation from the cold, and a heating stove, conveniences like the auto-tent became outmoded. The need to lug along utensils for meal preparation was now moot: cabins were frequently outfitted with miniature kitchens and equipped with all the pots and pans one would ever need for a day, week, or month of lodging.

At the outskirts of towns, near the major crossroads, and at strategic points along 66, entrepreneurs jumped into action. Farmers handy with a hammer and saw chopped down a grove of trees, threw up a half-dozen rustic cabins, and they were in business. Filling station operators slapped together a couple of native rock buildings out back and began renting them to the occasional customer stranded by mechanical problems. It seemed that everyone was trying to get in on a good thing—including the restaurants and cafes that already had an established clientele.

Within a few years, little white cabins that featured clapboard siding, exposed eaves, white picket fences, and flowering window boxes had changed the face of the Route 66 streetscape. Escape to the roadways now included personal privacy. The era of municipal camps was unofficially over—auto-camping was dead.

Suddenly, the rush to build sleeping units was on. In the years between 1929 and 1933, "more than 400,000 shacks for autoists" were erected nationwide. Because these units typically displayed a semi-circular or "U-shaped" arrangement with central office structure, common lawn area, and access to the bungalows by way of a dedicated driveway, they came to be known in the trade as "courts." Depending on the preference of the operators, a variety of adjectives were paired with the identifier

Signs of defunct motor courts abound along the Route 66 roadsides. Even after buildings and other structures have been stripped of their valuables, its the signs that often remain high above—isolated and protected from the vandals' hand. Near St. Clair, Missouri. *D. Jeanene Tiner ©1995*

144

resulting in signs that read "tourist court," "motor court," "cottage court," and a variety of similar combinations. Appropriately, the individuals that operated this style of lodging were called "courters."

Some of the courters doing business along the old highway took the Native American angle and extrapolated the possibilities to the limit. After World War II, Frank Redford surfaced as the undeniable king of the wigwam sleeper, erecting a pair of "Wigwam Villages" in the Route 66 towns of San Bernardino, California, and Holbrook, Arizona. In later years, a few imitators like the Motel Conway in El Reno, Oklahoma, tried to copy the eye-catching formula but never attained the same level of style.

Despite their appeal, fantasy structures did not rise to dominate the architectural philosophy of the motor court. By the late 1930s, industry publications

continued on page 148

Mr. and Mrs. J.D. Meredith owned and operated the Tower Court in Albuquerque, New Mexico, and entreated guests to stop "For Rest and Comfort" with their promotional postcards. Rooms in this Art Deco dream were completely modern and air-cooled: During the cold winter months, frigid air seeped through the windows and during the summer, evaporative "swamp coolers" pumped in a moist breeze. The technology required to create "refrigerated air" was still many years in the offing. *Author*

Regional styles of motel construction are typical along Route 66. In the southwestern states, facsimiles loosely based on the adobe brick architecture of the Pueblo Indians were once widespread. Back in the 1940s and 1950s, New Mexico became a bastion of the Pueblo cabin, with Albuquerque its capital. All along the commercial strip leading to and from the city center, tidy groups of squat, flat-roofed haciendas greeted the Route 66 motorist. *Preziosi Postcards*

Wally Byam's Amazing Airstream Clipper

"Speeding through a desert landscape full of sand and Joshua trees, it appeared to be an apparition streaking right out of a Buck Rogers serial!"

It was Wally Byam's dream to "place the great wide world at your doorstep, for you to yearn to travel with all the comforts of home." He knew there was a more satisfying way for motorists to travel with complete independence, wherever the road might lead. It was an ideal he realized by the creation of one of America's most gleaming icons: the venerable Airstream trailer.

The story of the silver legend began back in the late 1920s when Byam was making a living in the advertising field. He crossed over into the world of publishing and introduced several newsstand magazines, one concentrating on the do-it-yourself craze sweeping the nation. When he published an acquired article on the construction of a travel trailer, readers wrote in with complaints! The plans were unsound and impractical to build, leading Byam to initiate some backyard experimentation of his own.

After developing a workable design, he penned his own article outlining the assembly of an inexpensive, $100 trailer. When he offered booklets detailing the clever plans by mail, he was overwhelmed. Eventually, he improved his original concept and was doing a brisk business supplying pre-built units. With the success of a tear-drop-shaped, 13-foot, canvas and Masonite marvel dubbed the "Torpedo," he promptly dropped other career plans to manufacture trailers. With the belief that his unique models slipped along the byways "like a stream of air," he adopted the name "Airstream" in 1934.

Around the same time, aeronautical genius William Hawley Bowlus was busy developing a radically new trailer concept in the San Fernando Valley. As head of Ryan Aircraft's shop in 1927, he gained valuable expertise on the famed *Spirit of St. Louis* project. By the 1930s, he was riveting together a streamlined, monocoque fuselage—skillfully applying proven principles of aircraft design to the art of trailer construction. He called it the Bowlus Road Chief.

The important strength-to-weight ratio was optimized with an internal labyrinth of tubular steel frames providing a skeleton for structural panels of aluminum alloy. While most trailer configurations incorporated a bulky superstructure, the Bowlus model relied primarily on exterior skin panels for the distribution of stress loads. This skyworthy assembly technique improved overall resistance to flex and vibration, improving both mileage and towability.

In 1936, the January issue of *Trailer Travel* magazine featured a full-color illustration of the "Road Chief" on its cover. Speeding through a desert landscape full of sand and Joshua trees, it appeared to be an apparition streaking right out of a Buck Rogers serial! With its streamlined rooster-tail, Moderne windows, and polished aluminum, it was an aerodynamic embodiment of the future. Still, there was one design feature that didn't receive many accolades: the entry door. It was positioned at the front of the rig, right above the towing attachment!

Whether it was the door or the lack of marketing panache exhibited by Bowlus, the model failed to sell very well. Enter Wally Byam, part showman, part promoter—with his stockpile of advertising ideas and the pizzazz to make them work. After taking over the bulk of the Bowlus inventory, he relocated the entry and reintroduced the trendsetting trailer as the Airstream "Clipper." With the 1936 debut of the Bowlus cum Byam amalgamated streamliner, the machine age of transportation had arrived in style.

But, there was much more to the flashy trailers than mere aesthetics. Inside, the sleeper was built to accommodate four. Even seats converted into beds. A dinette of tubular frame was employed for dining and a diminutive galley to prepare food. An advanced heating and ventilation system (augmented by insulation) increased comfort—along with electrical lights, storage cabinets, and eight, fully opening side windows. Top-of-the-line models even included an experimental, dry-ice air-conditioning gizmo!

During the 1920s, trailer visionary Wally Byam found success with a tear-drop shaped, 13-foot, canvas-and-Masonite marvel dubbed the "Torpedo." Almost seven decades have passed, and today the travel trailer has evolved far from its humble beginnings. Motorhomes are now the perfect union between the automobile and the home, some featuring 118 gauges and instruments, the ability to store 400 gallons of fuel on board, microwave ovens, electrical beds, radar, satellite navigational systems, electronic maps, and even automatic leveling devices. *Courtesy of Airstream, Inc.*

When the war came, parts became difficult to obtain and aluminum was a critical war material. Consequently, Byam suspended Airstream operations and began work for a Los Angeles aircraft contractor. After the war, Airstream was taken out of mothballs and re-emerged stronger than ever to build the gleaming classics that made it an American original.

Today, the original Clipper, "old granddad" as it is now called, occupies a place of prominence in history—and the hearts of Airstreamers—at the company's headquarters in Jackson Center, Ohio. The graceful Airstream is a true survivor, one of only a handful of trailers made in America with the same standards of quality begun over 60 years ago. Wally Byam's vision and trailering dream is still rolling on!

The earliest RV'ers in America were a group of people who got together in 1919 in Sarasota, Florida. Known as the "Tin Can Tourists," they started with 22 families and within 10 years had grown to well over 100,000 members. They organized into camps, and suddenly southern towns found themselves in competition to host them. Much to the approval of businessmen, trailer people were interested in local events and boosted economies by purchasing food and supplies. As trailering gained in popularity, the appearance of overnight facilities featuring running water, bathrooms, and electricity made the lifestyle more appealing to the average family of the 1950s. In the postwar era, Americans rediscovered the joys of the open road. Many took to Highway 66 with their homes in tow and went off in search of the great American West. *Courtesy of Airstream, Inc.*

The Old Hotel Beale was Kingman, Arizona's, hub during the Roaring Twenties. Beneath the sleeping rooms were most of the services required by the lodger or guest just passing through. For buying ready-to-wear clothing goods, having one's hair cut, and even stocking up on cigars, it was one-stop shopping at its finest. The appearances of many small towns along Route 66, haven't changed all that much. Lieutenant Edward Fitzgerald Beale was a naval officer and explorer who surveyed a route from Fort Defiance (180 miles southwest of Santa Fe) to the Colorado River and California (with the assistance of camels) during the late 1850s. *Library of Congress*

continued from page 145

extolled a radical rethinking of the cabin and began outlining their ideas in print. Always eager to modernize, leading architects canonized the concepts of streamlining within the pages of *Tourist Court Journal*. The campaign worked.

Following the lead of service stations and Los Angeles drive-ins, courters accepted the ideas and began implementing an architectural facelift. Route 66 became a hotbed of style. In Carthage, Missouri, the Boots Motel emerged as a trendsetter by incorpo-

rating the rounded corners and speed lines favored by gas station architect Walter Dorwin Teague. But nothing could compare to the Coral Court in St. Louis: dominated by a minimalist rationale of ceramic tile and glass block, it was the quintessential incarnation of Streamline Moderne.

While the tourist cabins raced to upgrade, a new method for housing motorists began its slow encroachment on the business of lodging. Rumblings of the changes to come began as early as 1925

more contiguous structures. Arranged in a row parallel or perpendicular to the highway, rooms shared common walls—interrupted only by integral garage bays. Now, lodgers could back up to the front of a cubicle, pop the trunk, and unload baggage directly into the room. For the customer, the advantages of easy access were welcomed.

Even so, it was the roadside proprietor who came away with the best deal. With an

when architect Arthur Heineman designed an overnight establishment called the "Milestone Motels" in San Luis Obispo, California. The combination of the words "motor" and "hotel" spread quickly along the highway, providing a catchword to promote sleepers that looked like nothing more than elongated stables for cars.

By the mid-1950s, the villages of separate cabins that once decorated Highway 66 were replaced by

The Casa Linda was one of many motor courts influenced by the Indian Pueblo. Individual garage units were available for every room, but the lack of air-conditioning made visits during the hot months of summer a trial. When this photo was taken, Route 66 was still a dirt path through New Mexico. Gallup, New Mexico, G.B. Gordon photo. *National Archives*

The Coral Courts were a complex of 30 buildings (expanded to 77) that set a precedence for Moderne styling along Route 66. Built in 1941, they were designed by architect Adolph L. Struebig for the late Johnnie H. Carr, a colorful personality who was widely admired by the local community of Marlborough but held in dubious regard by the local police. Over the years, the Courts were the center of shady circumstances on a number of occasions. In October 1953, Carl Austin Hall stayed there the night before his arrest for the kidnapping and murder of Bobby Greanlease, the six-year-old son of a Kansas City auto dealer. The $300,000 ransom money that was paid him was never found—leading many to wonder if the hollow walls at the Coral Court may hold more than air. St. Louis, Missouri. *Shellee Graham ©1995*

With its close proximity to the Wal-A-Pai Indian Reservation, Kingman, Arizona's, Wal-A-Pai Court took full advantage of the Native American association. From the perspective of the present, it seems a bit ironic how poorly our nation has treated these indigenous people—yet freely exploited their words, images, and customs for use in commercial advertising and promotion. *Courtesy Chuck Sturm*

Vintage postcards depicting the Pueblo Bonito Court and the Koronado Kourts illustrate the contrasting styles of architecture employed by courters in various states along Route 66. In Joplin, Missouri, the overnight cottages are reminiscent of vacation bungalows whereas in Albuquerque the long strips of sleeping quarters evoke the visual and structural properties of the Native Pueblo longhouse. *Courtesy Chuck Sturm*

all-inclusive structure, motels provided a dramatic reduction in the amount of real-estate needed, as well as lower material and construction costs. Maintenance was cheaper, too. One maid could service a row of rooms in less time than it took to clean a sprawling layout of bungalows.

In the broad overview, it appeared that the simplified motel was the ideal solution for the traveling salesman, tourist, trucker, and highway adventurer of the modern motoring age. In reality, the motel was merely a

151

distant cousin of the early camps. Instead of the privacy afforded by one's own cabin, motels crowded patrons together in one building that had more in common with an impersonal military barracks than a resort. Surroundings were designed for efficiency—not relaxation.

Across the eight states connected by 66, the idea of a home-on-the-road had returned to one of communal togetherness. The blare

Lakeview Courts had it all: They were approved by the American Automobile Association, featured a cafe, had golfing facilities, boat rides, and were selected by restaurant reviewer Duncan Hines. Inside the rooms, things just got better with Simmon's Beds, Ace mattresses, electric refrigeration, and Magic Chef stoves! For the 1940s, these were roadside accommodations to write home about. Near Bethany, Oklahoma. *Courtesy Jerry Keyser*

from a television speaker and snore of a neighbor became modern replacements for the coyote's call. Lodging was now quick, convenient, and hassle free. Without any desire to linger, packing up the station wagon and speeding back onto Highway 66 became more important. In the rush to complete the journey, the special magic that was once associated with camping out along the American roadside was lost.

CORAL COURT
Ultra-Modern
One of the finest in the Mid-West on U. S. Highway 66 City Route, one mile west of City Limits, three miles east of intersection of By Pass, Highways #61, 66, 67 and 77

70 rooms, tile cottages with private tile bath in each room.
Hot and cold water porter and maid service
—Beauty Rest Spring and mattresses—
Hot Water Radiant Heat—24 Hour Service
7755 Watson Road (Highway 66)
St. Louis 19, Mo.

WOODLAND 2-5786

Desirous of a commercial structure that would require little maintenance, visionary John H. Carr chose hollow ceramic blocks manufactured by Architex Ceramics, Inc., of Brazil, Indiana, for the exterior of the now-demolished Coral Court Motel cabins. When applied as a veneer over standard concrete block, they made the outside walls of his Art Deco compartments one foot thick. St. Louis, Missouri. *Courtesy Chuck Sturm*

Hotel El-Rancho

TURNER TOURIST HOTELS, Inc.

E. W. TURNER, Pres.
Managing Director

GALLUP, NEW MEXICO -- ON U. S. HIGHWAY 66

The Hotel El Rancho was once known as "The World's Largest Ranch House." Accommodations for 250 guests made it one of the biggest operations catering to the tourist trade in the New Mexico area. Some of the more unusual features available there were cowboy bunks for the children and "sleeping porches" for the adults. Gallup, New Mexico. *Courtesy Chuck Sturm*

right
A street scene along the Atchison, Topeka, and Santa Fe railroad between Seligman, Arizona, and Needles, California. Note the commerce thriving along this urban strip: Lockwood's Cafe (with Chicken in the Rough sign), a Chevrolet car dealership, a Conoco gasoline outlet, the Hotel Beale, various bars, and other sundry stores. Kingman, Arizona, Jack Delano photo, 1943. *Library of Congress*

chapter five

IN appreciation of y
have arranged a
Automobile nee
ose for yourse

h a purchase of
aco Fire Chief R
asoline, you may
the following items.

FIRE-CHIEF GASOLINE

- Premiums
- Wash and Grease (with N
- Wash and Polish.
- Grease and Oil Change (
- Five Gallons of Texaco
- Oil change, Havoline Oi

WAGGONER'S SERV

ermak Rd.   Tel. (

ELI & SONS
5307 W. Cermak Rd.
Cicero 50 Ill.

Mother Road Memories:
Life on the Road

U.S. Route 66 is a highway made up of memories. It always has been. From the very early days of the blazed trails until the roadway's official birth during the 1920s and right on through the years leading up to its rediscovery during the 1990s, it has functioned as both an inspiration and a facilitator for an expansive realm of human experience. While intended to function as a purely utilitarian conduit for the purpose of car travel, the highway and its businesses have doubled as a base for memories.

While the various experiences of the millions of motoring Americans (and countless others from around the globe) who drove Highway 66 might be unique, a common thread of

Crossing the state line from Arizona to New Mexico along Highway 66 was a dramatic experience in 1940. Crowned with a Highway 66 shield, a massive portal welcoming newcomers to the state created an impressive sight for all those in the front seat. Of course, gasoline and curios (note small stand on lower left) awaited all those making a run for the border. Arthur Rothstein photo, 1940. *Library of Congress*

left
During the 1930s, Elias Kornblith ran Waggoner's Greasing Palace Number 33 in the Route 66 town of Cicero, Illinois. In addition to selling Crosley cars, they served a short order fare from a tiny lunch room on the parking lot. Up on their flashy sign, a young lady in a car was outlined in neon lights. To attract attention, her scarf flew up and down as the wheels on her vehicle turned. *Postcard and blotter courtesy Gordon Kornblith*

Jim Bragg reclines in the grass while preparing a peanut butter sandwich for a quick roadside lunch. While most of the couple's meals consumed while driving Route 66 were made with potted ham, fresh fish was an occasional treat. Bea caught her first fish in a river somewhere near old Route 66. *Photo courtesy Bea Bragg*

happenstance and incident bonds all of those who traverse its path. The incidents that take place upon this inanimate aggregate of concrete are universal. The problems encountered are endemic. The solutions found along the way are obvious. With little exception, the destinations reached, the locales visited, and the attractions viewed are all similar.

In most cases, the reasons for travel are related in both cause and purpose.

When viewed from a larger perspective, the resolution of each individual "trip" is less unique than actually perceived by its participants. Whether it be the migrant farm worker or displaced laborer seeking a new chance out west, the truck driver hauling products to market, vacationgoers packed into a station wagon, or a carload of insurance salesmen heading to a convention in Las Vegas, traveling along

Highway 66 eventually dictates a similar fate for all those who roll over its path.

Is there any dispute that all automobiles break down, radiators overheat, tires go flat, gas tanks run dry, and engines cease to spin? For the driver and his passengers, the schedule of events encountered during the journey is predictable: appetites must be quelled with food and occasional breaks be made for the rest room. Additional stops must be made for sleeping and also sights viewed. Money is spent, money is found, money is lost. Meanwhile, a tragic accident claims yet another victim. Inside the car compartment, people either get along famously or they spend their entire trip in pointless argument.

Nevertheless, this reality of the road's physical realm is quickly forgotten. More important in the long term are the lasting memories that are made along the way. Although the myriad of road-users who have driven this route represent diverse philosophies and lifestyles, the two lane slab of 66 has been—and continues to be—a point of intersection for a collective automotive experience. An American road experience. Within this continuum, new friendships are forged and old acquaintances revisited. Lost loves are found and old flames are rekindled. Thoughts are inspired and minds expanded. As motorists speed off to reach that distant vanishing point, new discoveries, adventures, disappointments, awakenings, and heartbreaks await. In the end, these are the elemental properties that real Mother Road Memories are made of.

We Found Our Road

You can't always find the right road on a map, but in 1939, two years after we were married, Jim and I found it: Route 66 from Oklahoma City to Los Angeles. It was more than just a road from here to there. On this road came joy and sadness. Our children were born nearby, and more than 50 years after our first anniversary, Jim died in Albuquerque near the old road.

War clouds were very dark that year. Rumors were strong that Hitler would invade Poland. More important to us newlyweds was that the Great Depression still lingered.

We lived in a $35 a month apartment in Oklahoma City with a living room so small our knees touched when we sat across from each other. We didn't mind that. Jim took $80 a month from his real estate business, and I earned 10 cents a page typing. We saved $125, ample for a three-week trip West to glamorous California or even east to wicked St. Louis or Chicago. The year before we had gone on family business to St. Louis, a well-known Route 66 stopover, but we went by train. We were still to experience the magic of Route 66.

At last, we would drive west toward the sunsets we watched from 39th Street, Route 66's path through the city. This would be our real honeymoon! Not like the weekend "honeymoon" after our wedding in 1937 which was—well, I can't tell you about that.

Our budget included gas at 12 cents a gallon for the 2,000-mile round trip. Our 1930 Chevy, which coughed above 40 (but was in good condition), got about 15 miles per gallon. Estimated expenses for the trip looked like this: gas, $16.00; motels (growing more plentiful westward), $1.50 to $3.00 per night; and food (for both of us), $1.00 a day. Anticipated total: $79.00. This left us with at least $45.00 for unforeseen expenses and perhaps one evening at a nightclub in Los Angeles! Wealth!

We packed 21 cans of potted ham, seven cans of tomatoes, and a can opener. Through dust storms in Amarillo, a cold spell in Gallup, and searing heat at Needles, we were sustained—mostly by excitement.

In Los Angeles we saw the museums and dipped our toes in the Pacific, but nothing could compare with the huge Hollywood nightclub. I must tell you, we were shocked! Sixty scantily-clad dancing girls had their bare backs painted with noses, mouths, and eyes. They faced the rear of the stage as they danced. That wasn't what shocked us. It was the one girl who was facing the audience, painted just like the others. Those who saw her—and of course, Jim did—roared with laughter. Everyone else was bewildered, for not all could see the dancing girl with wobbly eyes.

The International Golden State Exposition that year took us to San Francisco's Treasure Island. How could we have resisted? We were beginning to like potted ham! My biggest thrill? I got to type on a new product: an electric typewriter!

This momentous event rivaled a side trip on the way back home to Oklahoma City. Route 66 passed near Grand Canyon National Park. We had to go. With not much money and only two cans of potted ham left, we couldn't take expensive burro trips down into the canyon. We WALKED in, and WALKED out by sundown! The distance, 8-8/10 miles, seemed like 88 back!

Eagles soared and chipmunks chattered, but three people we met on that hike were the most curious of all. Jim, an avid camera fan, was curious about the famous Leica camera carried by the young man in front of us. A Leica! Almost in a class with the electric typewriter! Jim sprinted up to him. Their conversation was over in seconds. The youth stopped, turned to face Jim, raised his hand in a Nazi salute, and barked "Heil, Hitler!"

Jim stood stock-still, his jaw slacked in surprise, but our curiosity led us to persuade him to talk in his broken English. We learned that he was a Nazi student among hundreds traveling through the civilized world. All he would talk about was the "maliciously lying newspapers" in America.

At the bottom of the canyon, the student handed Jim his camera and indicated he wanted his picture taken. As Jim focused, the student clicked his heels, straightened his shoulders, and raised his hand in a Nazi salute. "Danke," he said, bowed, took his camera, and disappeared up the path.

Halfway out, we struggled for breath under a nut-pine tree. Two fellow hikers stopped to chat, asking questions about the Nazi. We got goose bumps when we learned they were FBI agents.

By 1940, we had a little better car and celebrated by driving Route 66 to Chicago where we saw Vivien Leigh, the controversial choice for Scarlett in *Gone With the Wind*, and Laurence Olivier in *Romeo and Juliet* on stage.

Jim and I traveled more widely in the years following, he to the South Pacific during World War II and, years later, both of us to Europe, Africa, Mexico, and Central America.

In 1991, we moved to Albuquerque, Route 66 country, where Jim died. Since his death, I have moved to an apartment where I can overlook Interstate 40, the highway that replaced Route 66. It leads to where Jim—and yes, I also, saw the girl with the wobbly eyes. The road where I touched the electric typewriter, where we saw George M. Cohan, Laurence Olivier, and Vivien Leigh, all gone now, and where the Nazi student and the FBI agents almost met.

Occasionally, as I watch the traffic, I think I hear our old Chevy coughing down Route 66.

—Bea Bragg

Marked for Life

Is it possible to "mark" a child, as old wives are fond of saying? My mother says my father "marked" me by threatening to move the whole family from Illinois to California while she was pregnant with me. She cried all day, every day, which she insists ensured that the child she carried would have the wanderlust my dad was never able to shake. As a result of Dad's need to travel, we moved often. I attended seven grade schools (including three third grades) and two high schools.

One trip I especially remember, however, took the family along Route 66. It was 1953, and I was five years old. Dad finally made good his threat and uprooted us from our home to move near his elderly mother in California.

Using his carpenter skills, Dad worked busily in the driveway, building what I believe to be the first camper—ever. On our old pickup truck, he constructed a frame of two-by-fours and covered it with chicken wire. Meanwhile, Mom did her part by giving away everything that wouldn't fit in the "camper." She hurriedly stuffed our clothing and other belongings into gunny sacks, which were placed in the bed of the truck and covered by a mattress. Other gunny sacks were attached to the sagging chicken wire overhead and, finally, canvas was draped over this lumpy, and obviously homemade, contraption.

Raymond Ryburn, Sr., with Theressa "Terri" Victor, David, and Raymond, Jr., pose for a snapshot in front of the camper that would become the Ryburn home during their 1953 Route 66 journey. To the left, Victor; Raymond, Jr.; David; Terri; and four-legged friends Spic and Span are pictured relaxing on the running board of an automobile—totally unaware of the traveling adventure the future holds. *Photos courtesy Terri Ryburn-LaMonte*

What didn't fit in the truck, Dad burned in a huge bonfire. Having not one sentimental bone in his body, he decided that toys took up too much room and promised that he would buy replacements when we arrived in California. Tearfully, I sacrificed my favorite and best loved "Linda" doll to the flaming funeral fire of practicality. My brothers were brave. They described our destination as a magical place where the sun shone every day, you never had to wear a coat, and you could pick oranges from the trees in your yard!

In preparation for our odyssey, Dad tied firewood to the running boards of the truck, and strapped two canvas water bags to the front for that long, hot trek across the desert. We were off for California on Route 66—a 2,000-mile adventure! We must have looked like the Joad family from *The Grapes of Wrath*. I was, of course, far too young to be embarrassed by our appearance, but I can now imagine what we looked like to others as we set off—canvas and children flapping in the wind!

Besides my dad, and Mom (who was pregnant and suffering from morning sickness), there were my three older brothers, Junior (who was car sick), David, Victor, myself (also car sick), my baby brother, Roger (who was in diapers), and our two dogs—Spic and Span. Dad spent more time waiting, sometimes patiently and other times not so patiently, at rest rooms, rest stops, and alongside the road than he did driving. The trip must have seemed an eternity for my dad—especially since the truck, at full ramming speed, couldn't have exceeded 35 to 40 miles per hour.

Route 66 was two lanes, bumpy, and very narrow. Rest stops were few and far between. A deluxe rest stop was an especially wide place in the road, a carved-up and falling-apart picnic table, and a 55-gallon drum for trash disposal. It was necessary, then, for obvious reasons, to stop at gas stations, and my brothers and I soon became rest room experts. Only Phillips 66 rest rooms met our exacting standards of cleanliness. At one gas station, however, we found a surprise. Victor and I each jerked open a door and found ourselves looking at each other across the toilet in the small room. Depending on which door you used, this particular rest room was either a boys' or girls'. The trick was to lock both doors once inside. We used up valuable time arguing about who was there first, but mom finally arrived to settle the issue, and ordered the boys out back.

Mom, the cleanest person in the world, spent all of her time fussing over us. She carried a washcloth in a bread wrapper and every time we stopped, she tried to clean us up, which was nearly a full-time job. As she washed faces and hands with cold water— the only faucet that ever worked—she would say, "We may be traveling, but there's no excuse for being dirty." We squirmed as she scrubbed our necks and then ran off to air dry while she turned to the next victim. I vowed that if I ever had children I would let them be as dirty as they wanted—I would never wash them!

Meals had a comforting sameness along the road. Dad stopped at a grocery store each morning for a package of cinnamon rolls or donuts and a half-gallon of milk. Of course, at every stop, he bought a paper cup of coffee to keep himself going. Lunch was a picnic: a hunk of bologna and bread to make sandwiches, milk, and if we were really good and Dad felt especially solvent, there might be cookies.

Some nights Dad kept driving; other nights he needed to sleep. One night, he found a quiet place near water to set up camp. He pulled the truck to the water's edge and unstrapped the firewood and pots and pans so that Mom could cook a hot meal. After dinner, my brothers spread a canvas under the truck where they slept. "Get to sleep you kids," was Mom's lullaby from the lumpy mattress she shared with Roger and me. Dad stretched out on the front seat of the truck and tried to sleep. I listened to the unaccustomed sounds of the night and thought I heard a mountain lion. I fell asleep hoping that Dad, the intrepid builder-of-campers and long-suffering trailblazer—or Spic and Span—would be able to save my poor, defenseless brothers. In the morning, my brothers were alive but covered with mosquito bites. I laughed at their splotchy appearance. After that, Dad was careful to choose camping places away from water!

In the back of the truck, we tried to entertain ourselves. We sang "California, Here I Come," over and over and over, that being the only line that we knew! We sang it with great gusto, however! Sometimes my brothers, who were older and more worldly, sang "Get Your Kicks on Route 66," imitating the sophisticated vocal stylings of Nat King Cole. They too were limited—having learned only the title verse to the song!

My brothers also entertained themselves by fighting. Once, when they jockeyed for position at the tailgate, Junior and David began to scuffle. Soon they were both hanging over the pavement. I just knew they would fall from the truck and be killed. I had never seen brains, and I had never seen them bashed out on the highway either. Victor shouted "Stop!" and I began to cry and pound on the cab of the truck. "Raymond, pull over," Mom barked. "We'll never get there at this rate, Hazel," grumbled Dad as he rolled to yet another unscheduled stop. Mom and Dad had mistaken my desperate pounding for "the call of nature." I blubbered the truth and my brothers denied it. "I don't know where you get these stories," scolded Mom. I vowed then and there that I would never try to save the lives of my lying, but very much alive, brothers again.

We pulled into San Bernardino at night and while the truck was being filled with gas by a friendly man in a uniform and bow tie, Dad got permission to stay overnight on their lot. I felt safer there; it was well lighted, but the sleeping arrangements were rather cramped. David, Victor, and I stretched out, almost full length, in the bed of the truck; Junior slept lengthwise against the tailgate. Mom and Dad couldn't have gotten much rest, sleeping upright in the front seat with Roger between them. Spic and Span took their places in the truck.

Although I was stiff and sore in the morning, I was grateful to be near the rest rooms—this was the most convenient place we had stayed. We stretched, yawned, and ate our customary road breakfast. Dad rolled up the canvas sides of the camper and tied them securely. "Kids, let's go," Mom shouted, counting aloud as we got into the back of the truck. "Five . . . okay, Raymond, we're all in." The truck began to roll toward the ocean. A slightly modified version of our favorite song wafted from the back—"California, Here I Am!"

I stuck my head out the side of the truck and let the air buffet my face. It was different than any air I had ever felt—warmer and moister, with a smell I would later identify as the ocean, although I had no idea what that might look like. But, I soon found out.

Dad stopped the truck at the beach; we had reached the end of Route 66. My brothers and I clambered over the tailgate and ran toward the water. I moved slowly as my bare feet sank into the sand. The waves made me gasp as they washed over my feet and the wet sand ran quickly from under my feet and back into the ocean. It was colder than I expected, and loud. I turned and looked back at the truck. Mom was holding Roger and shouting, "Get back from there! What are you boys doing?" My brothers had already found a beached jellyfish to torture. Dad walked toward me and I ran to hug him. In that moment, I didn't care if he ever replaced

my "Linda" doll. He had given me the road and the ocean! I was "marked" for life.

—Terri Ryburn-LaMonte

We Called Ourselves the Joy Boys

Looking back, it seems like we packed a lot of living into that golden summer of 1954. Of course, a year lasted longer then. In fact, some hours were interminable. We'd sit in class at Flagstaff High School and listen to the Santa Fe trains rumble through town. There were still mournful steam whistles mixed among the diesel air horns, and they all made us want to be anywhere but Flagstaff.

Not that Flagstaff was a bad place to grow up. But we were restless teenagers at the crossroads of Northern Arizona, where Route 66 and U.S. 89 intersected. We'd sit in a booth at the Round Up Cafe watching the world pass, daydreaming aloud of the time when we would join that passing crowd. Like many people in those postwar years, we Route 66 kids dreamed of California.

The Round Up was at the corner of Leroux Street and Santa Fe Avenue in downtown Flagstaff. Santa Fe, the Main Street in Flagstaff, was also U.S. 66, the Main Street of America.

In summer, cars were bumper-to-bumper on the narrow street: lots of older cars, of course, but also the boxy post-1949 Fords, bullet-nosed Studebakers, Buicks with portholes, Cadillacs with fins. You didn't see many foreign cars then. Sometimes the cafe was so crowded with travelers that the management didn't appreciate teenagers hanging out, nursing coffee or Cokes, and ogling the tourist girls.

But in winter, the cars were few and far between. Flagstaff sits at nearly 7,000 feet elevation, and sometimes 66 was icy, or slushy. Our resident highway patrolman had a sneaky patrol car, a white-over-maroon Ford hardtop with the white star stenciled on the off side, away from traffic. When things were slow, the cop tied down his buggy-whip antenna and baited out-of-state motorists into dragging Main Street. Then he'd nail them with the flashing lights installed in his grille.

We called ourselves the Joy Boys: Mark, Kirt, and I. Mark worked in gas stations and garages, of which Flagstaff had plenty, so he always had some sort of car. We'd pool money for gas and explore 66 as far as Holbrook, 90 miles to the east, or Ash Fork, 45 miles to the west.

With morbid fascination, we inspected mangled wrecks towed in from "bloody 66." Someone used to put a white cross at the scene of each traffic fatality; the shoulders of some dangerous intersections, like Cottonwood Wash east of Winslow, looked like veterans' cemeteries!

After we graduated from high school in 1953, my three buddies moved to the Los Angeles area and got jobs. My parents set a lot of store in my getting an education, so I entered tiny Arizona State College at Flagstaff, now Northern Arizona University. But at the end of my freshman year, I couldn't stand it any longer. I had to see what lay beyond Ash Fork.

Jim Cook (pictured third from the left), Bob Atkinson, Mark McGrew, and Kirt Hart called themselves the Joy Boys. They discovered Route 66 and headed out to Los Angeles, California, in 1953 to get jobs. When they weren't on the beach, they spent a lot of time in a variety of automobiles (some with major mechanical problems) hanging out on Colorado Boulevard and cruising the Main. *Photos courtesy James Cook*

I soon found out that the first thing that lay beyond Ash Fork was one long, long day. I caught a ride with a college buddy who was going home to Los Angeles for the summer. He had a 1936 Ford coupe with a cracked head. We stuffed our belongings into the little car, along with a Jeep-can of water and a few cans of oil.

That day, I was introduced to Seligman, Peach Springs, Truxton Canyon, Valentine, Hackberry, then the long, straight drive across the plains to Kingman. A couple of years earlier, the "Grapes of Wrath" road had been pulled out of Goldroad and Oatman. The newer, straighter Route 66 went south from Kingman around the end of the Black Mountains, then bent west toward Topock, following the Sacramento Wash.

Today, it is fashionable, or at least politically correct, to admire deserts. But crossing the Mojave that first time, I concluded that the supply of desert exceeded the demand (the last time I drove that area, traveling Interstate 40 in an air-conditioned Buick in the summer of 1992, I had the same feeling).

West of Needles, Route 66 veered south of today's Interstate 40 to touch Essex and Amboy, tiny oases on that long, bleak road. Amboy was one of the several places we stopped to put more water in the Ford and add a little oil. We pressed on through Daggett and Barstow. It was night when we got to Victorville, and near midnight when we cruised along Colorado Boulevard into Pasadena, where my buddies were living.

I moved in with Mark and Bob and they got me a job at the factory where they worked; Kirt lived alone in Glendale and

worked in a bakery. I was in Pasadena two days before the smog cleared enough to show me the San Gabriel Mountains towering over the metropolis. At the factory, I worked days, spending the summer polishing the heads of tiny screws that went into drafting machines. But, the nights and weekends were ours to roam the wonders of the big, sprawling Los Angeles complex.

Being young and full of vinegar, we adapted quickly to the frenetic L.A. lifestyle, driving long distances on boulevards and freeways to find a beach or a concert. The Joy Boys spent a lot of time hanging out at one of the three original Bob's Big Boy drive-ins on Colorado Boulevard (these hip teenage hangouts eventually evolved into today's J. B.

The Horn Brothers Gas Station was a Route 66 landmark at 5418 East Central Avenue in Albuquerque, New Mexico. In 1946, Otho Driskill (near the pump) and station worker Manuel sold a White grade of gasoline at 15-1/2 cents and a Bronze grade at 17-1/2 cents per gallon. Six gasoline pumps widely spaced on a narrow gravel driveway allowed for high sales volume. *Photos courtesy Glen Driskill*

restaurants). Mark had a picturesque 1941 Plymouth sedan, painted primer gray. Its single exhaust pipe had a glass-pack muffler that gave it a throaty roar; most of the time, we couldn't get it into low or reverse gear, which resulted in some creative driving.

On weekends, we went to the beaches and baked ourselves in the sun. We danced to Les Brown's Band of Renown at the Hollywood Palladium and bought records in the round Capitol Records store on Hollywood Boulevard. Lynn, Mark's girlfriend, sat on my 78-rpm recording of Ray Anthony playing "As Time Goes By," and I've been trying to replace it ever since. We listened to "Sh-Boom," the original rock 'n' roll song that came out that summer. That first version, by The Chords, and the quick cover by The Crew Cuts, was all over L.A. radio. It was a novelty, and we never figured it to last.

I met a petite girl named Anne, whose brown hair was bleached by the California sun. We spent some pleasant, innocent times together. We held hands, necked at drive-in movies, and stumbled around a dance floor or two. We not only didn't get to first base, but weren't sure where the ballpark was.

Looking back from long perspective, I think I made two good decisions that summer. The first was going to Los Angeles; I might not have made the trip that gave new depth to my life. The second good decision was going back to Flagstaff and college.

Mark needed to tie up loose ends in Flagstaff so he could go into the Air Force. We left Pasadena at midnight to avoid some of the August heat across the desert. Mark drove hard to Needles, where we had breakfast at dawn. Unfortunately, when I started the Plymouth after breakfast, we heard an unmistakable knock. "Oh boy," Mark said, or words to that effect, "she's about to throw a rod!" I nursed the Plymouth along Route 66 at 35 miles per hour, hoping the piston connecting rod didn't let go. It didn't, but that was a long trip from Needles to Flagstaff.

We never heard from Bob again after that summer. Mark and Kirt have lived in Southern California for a long time. Mark and I keep in touch, and we hear from Kirt once in a blue moon. My wife died in 1991 and Kirt's in 1993. Anne visited Flagstaff one weekend in 1955 and later enrolled at ASC. She married a guy named Bob Cook, and they're still happily married. Bob's not related to me, but Anne says if she hadn't met me, she wouldn't have met him. So, the summer of 1954 was a watershed in her life too.

A couple of years ago, Anne asked me to autograph a book I had written "to the dumbest California girl I ever knew!" I changed that to "the most innocent California girl . . ."

—James E. Cook

Horn Brothers Gasoline

In the summer of 1945, I sat on an old wooden bench with my dad and Manuel, one of his gas station employees, drinking an R.C. Cola. We watched as the traffic moved through Albuquerque along U.S. Highway 66. The highway ran straight from Tijeras Canyon to the east, through town, and then up Nine Mile Hill to the west. People were on the move during the last year of World War II.

My dad's Horn Brothers station at 5418 East Central was typical of the independent stations of the 1940s. It had six pumps widely spaced along a narrow gravel driveway. A large sign above the driveway proclaimed "HORN BROS." and underneath, "never undersold!" Smaller signs attached to the single large light pole which lit the driveway at night advertised gas prices to back up the claim: "White" at 15-1/2 cents, "Bronze" at 17-1/2 cents.

As we relaxed in front of the station, a 1928 Pontiac, moving slowly west, made a left turn into our driveway, the car's wooden spoke wheels creaking under the heavy load. The engine side access doors were folded under the top part of the hood to help cool the hot motor. Mattresses and bed springs were tied to the top and all kinds of luggage and household items were strapped to the back over the rear bumper. A spare tire with an nasty looking bulge in the sidewall rode atop the luggage. The driver, a haggard looking man, shared the front seat with a tired, stringy-haired woman nursing a baby. Four kids with unkempt white hair hung out the rear windows. The car stopped at a pump marked "Bronze."

"What'll it be, mister?" my dad asked as he approached the car

"What's this here Bronze gas?" the man asked.

"It's white gas with lead added. It's cheaper than Regular and the lead keeps the engine from knocking."

"I'll take a gallon of it. And I'll need this here can filled up with kerosene."

Dad put in a gallon of gas and Manuel took the five-gallon can to the back and filled it with kerosene. "That'll be 18 cents for the gas, 50 cents for the kerosene and a gallon ration coupon," Dad said as he returned to the car.

Reaching deep into the back pocket of his tattered overalls, the man pulled out a small leather coin purse and counted out 68 cents, then dug a tattered government issue Rationing Book from another pocket. His large weathered hand fumbled nervously as he tore out a coupon, leaving only six.

"Where you headin'?" my dad asked.

"We're trying to get to California. We've gone broke farming in Oklahoma. We heard there's jobs in the war plants out in Los Angeles. We sold everything 'cept what we're carrying."

As he pulled out onto Highway 66, my dad said, "Watch what he does now!" Dad had seen it many times before. The man drove a hundred yards down the road, pulled over and poured the five gallons of kerosene in the gas tank of the car. He then drove to the Iceberg Cafe and Gas Station to repeat the process. He had to fill his tank with kerosene in Albuquerque so he could make it to Gallup. He did not have enough ration stamps to buy gas all the way to California and it was illegal for gas station operators to sell kerosene for cars. The old cars with low compression engines would run on kerosene if they were started on gasoline and kept warm.

"I'd like to help that feller out, but I ain't got nothin' either," Dad lamented as he returned to the bench.

A steady stream of cars passed the station during the day. Many of the cars carried poor farm people heading west along Highway 66. They were the tail end of the "Great Migration" which had peaked during the Dust Bowl years of the 1930s as described by John Steinbeck in *The Grapes of Wrath*. Everyone going either east or west, except the few who took the northern route, passed along the narrow two-lane paved road known as U.S. Highway 66. Most of the towns in the West were built along Highway 66 which for much of the way, was also the route of the railroads. Everyone traveling the highway had to plow laboriously through the traffic and slow speed zones in each town on the way. Many of the towns' economies were based on tourism which blossomed after World War II. Albuquerque set the pattern for the towns. The highway through town was a 20-mile stretch from the Sandia Mountains in the east to the steep climb up the West Mesa. Small motels, curio stores, bars, and greasy spoon restaurants lined the road.

During World War II, the government attempted to restrict travel by rationing gasoline and tires in order to conserve oil and rubber resources for the war effort. It didn't stop the migration of starving people from the farms of Oklahoma and other states still feeling the effects of the Great Depression. The ones left out of the war effort as soldiers because of physical or family situations had to move where the jobs were—the flourishing West Coast war industries.

Many of the people who came through Dad's station were hungry, tired, and broke.

They were risking everything to get to California. They couldn't afford to buy tires and didn't have ration stamps to buy them anyway. Dad sold "boots" to be installed between the inner tube and the tire to cover the holes in the tire. Tubes were patched and repatched until they looked like checkerboards. People carried canvas drinking-water bags which were cooled through evaporation.

We sold bulk oil from barrels because it was cheaper, and we drained the empty bulk oil bottles and cans into a waste can so we could sell the drippings cheaper still. Desperate people would try to barter anything they had to get what they needed to complete their trip. Dad had a soft heart and managed to secret away a few ration stamps that "fell through the cracks." He used them to help a few of the most desperate people.

Native New Mexicans from the other side of the mountains, east of the Sandias and Manzanos, were also feeling the pinch of dried-up farmland. Some were moving to Albuquerque for work, but many were sticking it out—waiting for the return of seasons of even sparse rain; adequate for the western technique of dry farming beans and potatoes. Dad provided them with credit for gas and oil. Much of the money was not repaid,

The U-Drop Inn has evolved to become one of the most popular standards along Highway 66 in West Texas. John and Bebe Nunn were the original operators of the restaurant, which they sold in the 1940s, then repurchased in 1950. They renamed the landmark Nunn's Cafe and set upon the task of feeding the throngs of back road adventurers in search of the past. Today, it is a "must see" and "must eat" stop along the Texas track of Highway 66. Shamrock, Texas. *Dan Harlow ©1995*

Joe Morrow (posed by the truck with his wife, Leta) relied on the business of trucking for a livelihood. In 1950, he bought his own rig and operated as a "wildcatter." Hauling freight and produce all over the United States, Route 66 was always a part of his trips. For him, the highway was an economic "lifeline." His brother, Jewell, (now deceased) and wife, Brownie, (posed with a Tydol Gasoline sign) ran the family gas station after their father, George Morrow, passed away. *Photos courtesy Joe Morrow*

which contributed to my dad's parting with the Horn Brothers.

For many years, the only other structure near the station was the Iceberg Cafe and Gas Station, located across the highway and a few hundred yards west (now the corner of Central and San Mateo). The Iceberg Cafe was fabricated from wood and metal lath and plastered to look like a large iceberg rising from the stark desert. The cafe and a smaller iceberg used for the station office were landmarks for many years. The two were later moved and unceremoniously dumped out near Bernalillo, where they sat for many years before being destroyed. The Tewa Motor Lodge was built across the highway from the station in 1946. Dad's station was torn down in 1955 to make way for the Trade Winds Motel. A Chinese restaurant now occupies the site.

Thinking of that station on Highway 66 reminds me that the "good old days" were not so good for some people, but their move West made it better for their children.

—Glen W. Driskill

My Route 66 Lifeline

When I was a small boy my dad bought three acres of land on Route 66, west of Springfield, Missouri. He built a service station complete with living quarters alongside the highway.

The place was built out of beautiful, native worm fossil rock. Inside was a large room with shelves and a counter with stools where travelers' supplies, such as bread, milk, and candy were sold. He had planned to build six or eight cabins for tourists (that was before the word "motel" was in the dictionary). He completed two cabins before ill health stopped his project. The doctors referred him to the Mayo Clinic in Rochester, Minnesota. He died there in 1935. After Dad passed away, my oldest brother took over the operation of the station and the cabins.

During my childhood I was fascinated by the big trucks that went by our home and our station. To me they were huge, though they were only single-axle tractors and single-axle trailers, nothing like the giant rigs of today.

I found an old pair of steel roller skates that someone had discarded and took the front rollers off of one skate and hooked it on the other skate. Hey, I had myself a trailer truck! I cherished that homemade toy for a long, long time and never did get over my fascination for the big trucks.

I enlisted in the Navy on my 17th birthday, near the end of World War II, and was discharged in 1948. I got a job driving a truck for a creamery company that had a government contract to supply milk to Fort Leonard Wood. Seven days a week, Springfield to Fort Leonard Wood, all on Route 66.

In 1950, I bought my own tractor-trailer rig and operated as what we used to call a "wildcatter." I hauled freight and produce all over the United States, but almost everywhere I went, Route 66 was a part of the trip, because Springfield was my home. Many times I loaded in Chicago for a haul to California and vice versa, heading along old Route 66 all the way. There were other routes I could have taken—the northern or southern routes—but for me it was always 66. I could stop at home, get rested, grab some clean clothes, or a home-cooked meal before hitting the road again.

In 1956, I went out of business. I always considered myself to be a good driver and figured if I had an accident it would be the other guy's fault. So when I paid off the rig, I dropped my collision insurance because it was very expensive. Well it didn't turn out as I had planned. Yes, I had an accident. Yes, it was my fault. I ran into the back of another truck. And, yes, it was on Route 66, just outside of Hamel, Illinois.

I got a job driving for Powell Brothers Truck Line. Most of the runs were from Springfield to St. Louis—good old 66 again. Then I drove for Voss Truck Lines, whose home office was in Oklahoma City. They moved freight between Chicago and Oklahoma City—yep, Route 66! In 1960, Voss sold out to Western-Gillette, which had its home office in Los Angeles, and in 1977, Western-Gillette sold out to Roadway Express. I retired in 1985.

I have no way of calculating how many miles, hours, days, or even years of my life have been spent on Route 66. I know the old highway contributed a great deal to my source of income and livelihood. I believe I can truly say, "Route 66 was my Lifeline."

—Joe Morrow

Waggoner's Greasing Palace

My father, Elias Kornblith, had the idea that anything a friend of his could do, he could do just as well. So, he jumped headfirst into the business of selling refined petroleum—just like his friend Phil Sloan, a man who started in the gas station business from scratch in the pre-Depression late 1920s. Sloan teamed up with his brother and managed to amass a large number of gasoline outlets and in the process inspired my dad to take action.

Eager to get started, my father asked his brother to be his partner, and after soliciting a loan from my uncle's father-in-law, they constructed a sprawling gasoline station that featured five grease pits, a car wash large enough to handle four cars at the same time, and a brake shop with three service stalls. Out front, they put in a big parking lot so there would be enough space for a large number of cars.

To the locals—and all the other customers filling their tanks before venturing out onto Route 66—the business was known as Waggoner's Greasing Palace Number 33. Don E. Waggoner was the regional sales manager for the refueling operation, and consequently, all of the gasoline stations used his name for many years after that.

Well, although Dad and his brother didn't amass a large number of stations like Sloan and company did, they managed to pump more gasoline than anyone else in the entire area. During the 1930s, the increased competition from gas wars and labor strikes didn't hurt them a bit. They simply set their gas prices ridiculously low and concentrated their efforts on top-quality service. As fast as the delivery tankers could off-load the fuel into their station storage tanks, it was sold.

Clever marketing was part of the great sales success: Open 24 hours a day, Waggoner's Greasing Palace gave out a premium of four quarts of motor oil with every eight gallons of gasoline purchased. The public response to the gimmick was so good that not only were enthusiastic customers filling their auto tanks with fuel—they were taking some extra liquid home in a variety of portable containers!

After the first week, the Cicero, Illinois, fire chief begged my father to stop the promotion and to take heed of the fact that people were going home and draining their car tanks into 55-gallon barrels. As he figured it, all across the suburbs of Chicago, motorists were hoarding hundreds of gallons of gasoline in their garages. "One spark and the whole town would burn for a week!" was his worried warning.

Originally, Dad opened the gas station as a Texaco. After buying his brother and the other partners out, he switched to the colorful brand of the Flying Red Horse. Of course, the company that would one day become Mobil was still known as Socony-Vacuum back then, the result of the giant Standard Oil conglomerate merging with the much smaller Vacuum Oil Company. For business, it was a wise switch. Through the experience of servicing all the Western Electric Company service trucks, we found out that the quality of Socony-Vacuum oil products were very consistent. Not surprisingly, we later realized that Mobil Oil products were always on a higher plane than most of the other brands.

Fortunately, the Mobil name not only proved to be a mark of quality, but one perfect for all types of promotion. With that in mind, Dad asked a man by the name of Zed Gerwe (Illinois head of the Mobil Oil Company) to install something more attention-getting in place of the porcelain enamel shield sign that represented Socony-Vacuum. The following week, Dad got his wish. Gerwe delivered an immense, blazing Red Pegasus outlined in bright neon! It was exactly what Dad had in mind: an attention-getting billboard that plainly illustrated the ideas of speed, flight, and horsepower.

Unfortunately, even the powerful red horse could not stop the march of time and progress. Those unforgettable days of wiping the windows and checking the oil were bound to end sometime. And end they did!

My brother and I sold the Greasing Palace property in 1979, and the gallant red steed that once greeted car customers was taken down and retired.

Even so, the memories remain strong. To this day I still have many friends who remember the good old days. Back then, I could actually call all of the customers by their first names and watch as their children grew up to drive (and follow) in their footsteps. Although the town of Cicero, Illinois, and the many events that made history there are slowly slipping into obscurity, the sign of the Flying Red Horse remains as a vibrant reminder of the golden age when gas stations were called greasing palaces and station attendants pumped the gasoline.

—Gordon Kornblith

We Almost Made It

In 1950, the Korean War was escalating. As a 19-year-old facing possible military draft, all I really wanted to do was experience the ultimate driving/sightseeing adventure—Chicago to Los Angeles on Route 66. There were still some rough, narrow, desolate roads to challenge the traveler, and no car air-conditioning, superhighways, motel and fast food chains, credit cards or jet airliners to pamper him. Often, there were lengthy stretches along which no radio stations could be picked up.

On the plus side, gas was 20 cents a gallon, Cokes and candy bars were a nickel, and motels could be found for $5 a night. Best of all, the posted speed limit was often 70 miles per hour, and in some places there were no signs, which meant any speed that was "reasonable and proper."

My father died that summer and as the only licensed driver in the family, I got his 175,000-mile 1941 Buick Century to use as my own. With its dual compound carburetors it easily hit 30 in first gear and 60 in second. And boy, was I anxious to discover the top speed. When driven reasonably, it would deliver 18 miles per gallon on the highway.

My friend Harvey Mayer and I scraped together a total of $125, packed three dozen cookies my sister baked for us, and jumped on Route 66 where it began, at Michigan and Jackson in Chicago. Due to youthful impatience, we wanted to see Los Angeles as soon as possible, so we drove over 1,000 miles straight through to Amarillo, Texas. We stopped only for gas, washrooms, milk for the cookies, and unfortunately, tires.

Our persistent car trouble began in St. Louis when I noticed that what had been perfectly good front tires when we left were now very badly worn on the edges to the point where the rubber was gone and the interior cords were exposed. They were unsafe and

Ken Greenburg poses with the familiar "Arizona Welcomes You" sign at the border of New Mexico. With friend Harvey Mayer, Greenburg crossed the continent in the year 1950 driving a 1941 Buick Century fraught with tire problems. Although the team ultimately had to turn back before getting to California, they both realized that the journey is often more important than the destination. *Photo courtesy Ken Greenburg*

useless, so we bought two pair of used tires for three dollars each. At the same time, a mechanic examined the front end and pointed out all the worn parts that made it impossible to align the car. It needed a major repair with new parts at a cost we could in no way afford. Relying on our youthful wisdom again, we decided to keep heading west and to watch the tire wear very carefully and buy more used tires as needed.

We looked around in Springfield, Missouri, and took some pictures, with my oddball Whittaker Micro 16 miniature camera. We then sped on to Tulsa where we had to buy two more tires. The oil wells pumping all over the place were fascinating. It was either in Missouri or Oklahoma where we saw our first red dirt, which became red mud in the rain and really stuck like glue to the car. So far, the drive had been mostly boring. We wanted to see mountains, desert, and mostly, jump into the Pacific Ocean. The flatlands did not capture our imagination.

I did most of the driving, and because it was an old car, I usually kept the speed under 75. However, much to my unhappy concern, when Harvey drove and I dozed, he kept the needle at 85 or 90. We argued about this a lot, and I let him drive less and less. I was driving somewhere in Oklahoma, when a front tire disintegrated, causing us to leave the road, crash through a thin wire fence and finally bounce to a stop several hundred feet into a field! We were lucky the car didn't flip over.

Still shaking from the near miss and driving a little slower, we got to Amarillo very tired. There we bought three more tires, had another mechanic look at the front end, and he gave us the same dire diagnosis. This was our first night in a motel or as they were called then, a motor court. After a good night's sleep, we looked around the city, and all I can remember was that a lot of people were wearing cowboy boots and hats. It was obvious we were tourists.

As we drove to Albuquerque, the scenery was definitely getting more interesting. We could see the great Rocky Mountains way off in the distance. Now the adrenaline was beginning to flow. In Albuquerque, we bought two more tires and some kind of canvas-covered water bag to hang on the front bumper like everyone else was doing, I guess in anticipation of crossing the desert. The hills began getting steeper and taller and from the top of each one, all we could see was an endless ribbon of concrete seemingly vanishing into infinity.

As the road grades got increasingly steeper, I nervously watched the temperature gauge climb dangerously close to the overheat point, but with much relief, I watched it recede to normal on the way down. We began seeing signs telling drivers to shift to a lower gear when going downhill.

At last, we arrived in Gallup, which was not very much at that time. We slept in our second motel there. The drive from Gallup to Flagstaff was uneventful, but the scenery was improving all the time. I don't remember anything about Flagstaff except that the ride from there to Kingman was brutally hot—115 degrees was not uncommon and at 75 miles per hour the air felt like it was exiting a blast furnace. It was oppressive and very uncomfortable. I knew it was best to travel at night when it's that hot, but we just couldn't wait to see California. I clearly remember in a remote area seeing signs advertising water for 25 cents a gallon. The heat made us cranky and at this point we began getting on each other's nerves.

When we got to Needles, we took stock, looked at our expense record, and realized that food, gas, motels, and tires had used up more than half our money. We could in no way make it to Los Angeles and back home on less than $50! With great sadness, we had to start back home without even seeing the Pacific Ocean.

There are several postscripts to this story: When we got home, Harvey discovered his Army Reserve unit had been activated the day we left. Within a month, he was shipped to Korea. I finished college and one week after I graduated, I was drafted into the Army. A major disappointment was that all the many pictures I took were either lost or more likely intentionally destroyed, because I had unwittingly mailed cash along with the film to be developed! That film could only be developed by the company in Los Angeles that had manufactured the camera. It was heartbreaking. I don't know what happened to all the pictures Harvey took with his camera. The photo of me by the Arizona sign is the only one I have from our trip.

On a brighter note, in 1955, on my honeymoon, I finally drove Route 66 all the way to the Santa Monica Pier, this time in a 1946 Buick Roadmaster. Things were beginning to change along the old road, but it was still a wonderfully romantic drive, and people along the way were still universally friendly and helpful to tourists. A few years after that, my wife and I made the drive one more time in a new station wagon with our two young kids who complained, whined, and fought most of the way. But, that's another story.

—Ken Greenburg

The Fearless Foursome

They were not Tod and Buz in a Corvette nor the Joad family in a truck escaping the Oklahoma dust bowl. Nor were they Thelma and Louise in a Thunderbird headed for disaster. They were just Mildred, Emily, Lucille, and Hazel, four young women who left Clear Lake, Iowa, in 1932 aboard a Model T Ford

Mildred Pattschull (above right) hitched up with three friends and drove a 1925 Model T Ford across the country in 1932. Although the rickety bucket-of-bolts cost her only $75, the car (middle frame) made it to California in just 10 days! Mildred is pictured behind the steering wheel with her friends Emily, Hazel, and Lucille looking on. *Photos courtesy Mildred Pattschull*

175

Chicago, Illinois, was the point of origin for Highway 66 and holds the distinction of supplying the eastern portion of the road with plenty of automobiles. It still does. John Vachon photo, 1941. *Library of Congress*

with a madcap idea to take a road trip on Route 66 to California.

"At first I really didn't have a strong desire to go," said Mildred Pattschull, now 82. "California seemed like a million miles away at the time. But my three friends were just dying to go, so I finally agreed to drive my car until it quit running. Then we would scrap it and come home."

As luck, or fate would have it, the 1925 Model T Touring car, purchased two years earlier for $75, was up to the task. It took them from Mason City, Iowa, to Los Angeles and back with few problems, a total of 3,900 miles!

Not many people made such trips in 1932, especially young single girls. Most women didn't even drive at that time, let alone take off on their own. And, to spend hard-earned cash during the Depression on a zany motor trip

would have been considered a foolish idea by many.

But not to Mildred. She was a spunky forerunner of independence and freedom before feminism was a movement. Mildred was simply too busy being Mildred, a person on her own road of discovery.

"My mother was convinced she'd never see me again," said Pattschull. "Both my parents openly cried in the front yard of our home the day we drove away. They just didn't understand."

She was just 20 years old. Today's equivalent might be the shock a parent would experience if a daughter announced her intent to canoe across the Atlantic Ocean. After all, most roads in America then were rutted dirt lanes with few services. And the Wild West was still considered, well, wild. But, Mildred and her friends were out to "get their kicks on 66," which in 1932 was still more a gravel path than paved highway.

Mildred's Model T Ford—a cramped, narrow, rickety-bucket-of-bolts had no windows, side curtains, or reliable tires—let alone air-conditioning, stereo, or cellular phone. She had driven the car for two years and named it "Ben Hur." It didn't have a top, but she found one just before they left.

"In the winter, I just piled on more clothes," explained Pattschull. "And I'd turn the seat upside down to keep the snow off while it was parked outside." Pattschull grew up in Iowa where winters are notoriously cold and windy.

The four young women—ages 19 to 22—drove south on Iowa Highway 65 through

Missouri and Kansas and hooked up with Route 66 at Oklahoma City. "We each had $100 cash," related Pattschull. "It was an enormous sum with the Great Depression descending hard on everybody. I don't even remember how we were able to accumulate that amount, but we did!"

Back then, however, meals in restaurants cost around 25 cents. Mildred's diary of the trip lists every dime she spent. One entry is for a bowl of chili at 15 cents and another is for a roast beef dinner for 35 cents. Gasoline was about 20 cents per gallon.

The group stayed in tourist cabins along the way—the forerunner of motels—for $1 per night! Each unit was only a small single room with a bed. Showers were in a separate building and the toilets were outhouses. All four young women slept in one double-bed—two at the head and two at the bottom with their legs intertwining at the middle. It was cheaper to rent one cabin and they felt safer being together.

Even though the song "Get Your Kicks on Route 66" (made famous by Nat King Cole) had not yet been written by Bobby Troup, Mildred and her friends "motored West and took the highway that's the best." They went through Oklahoma City ("looking mighty pretty"), Amarillo, Gallup, New Mexico, Flagstaff, Arizona, ("don't forget") Winona, Kingman, Barstow, and San Bernardino. They left Mason City May 28, 1932, and arrived in Los Angeles on June 7—11 long days of driving. They had little human contact on vast stretches of empty road between towns and road conditions

kept "Ben Hur" chugging along faithfully, mile after hot dusty mile, at about 20 miles per hour. Arizona had only been a state for 20 years when they drove through it, and the population was numbered less than Iowa's—fewer than 500,000 people.

"There was nothing—not one living thing—except sagebrush and sand along much of our trip," exclaimed Pattschull. "It was a real no-man's land, and it took about three hours to drive between any signs of civilization—if you could call some of these tiny towns along the way civilization."

The burning sun and the hot winds of the southwestern desert forced two of the women to wear men's long sleeved work overalls and drape a bath towel over their heads to protect their skin. Their only real brush with trouble came in Las Vegas, New Mexico, when they took a wrong turn and ended up in an unfamiliar neighborhood.

"All the signs were in Spanish, which we couldn't read, and we ended up on a one-way, dead-end street," Mildred recalled. "We apparently made an illegal U-turn and got arrested by a Spanish-speaking policeman and hauled off before some magistrate and a young teenage interpreter!" Ordered to appear the next morning in court, they got up at 4:00 a.m. and made a quick getaway out of town in the dark.

They all marveled at the lush green valleys and bright blue skies around San Bernardino after driving so long in the desert. They were especially impressed with the thousands of orange groves in that area and the limitless clear blue skies. The term smog had yet to be coined!

"It just seemed there were millions of orange trees everywhere," said Pattschull. "People had them in their front and back-yards and there were roadside stands selling oranges and juice." In a picture postcard sent to her parents during the trip, Pattschull said, "I would love to live on the beach in California or in some parts of Arizona. We all like it in New Mexico."

One of their foursome is now deceased, but the other three continue to be close and frequently write and telephone one another. Hazel Mitchell died in 1984. Emily Abbott lives in Glendale, California, and Lucille Lackore lives in Winona, Minnesota. "We never lost touch with each other," said Mildred, "but we didn't all get back together for a reunion until five years ago. We relived the entire trip, of course, and laughed and howled over our memories.

"I'd love to do that trip all over again today," said Pattschull as she sat behind the wheel of a 1921 Model T Touring car owned by Tom Wick of Clear Lake, Iowa. She hadn't gripped a steering wheel like this one since the day she sold Ben Hur in 1933—the year she got married. "That trip was a highlight of my life," exclaimed Pattschull, beaming a wide smile through the windshield. "I can feel the memories roll over me. Even though we were only gone a month, I felt as if I'd been transformed into adulthood when we got back."

—Jay Black

Patterson's Route 66 Milk Run

When I was nine years old, my family was preparing for a two-week automobile trip to see my father's relatives in California. It was going to be the first (and last) major vacation the entire family—my mom, dad, and three brothers—would take from our dairy farm in Augusta, Kansas. In preparation for the trip, mom got us all excited by showing us literature, maps, and other things about where we were going and what we could see along the way. I was pretty excited and so were my brothers Dalton, seven, and Allen, three.

But before we could leave, my mom and dad (Clare and Jessie Patterson) had to get someone to take care of the dairy farm and make sure that our registered Holsteins were kept in good shape. After some searching for qualified caretakers, Dad hired local boys Bill and Peewee Duncan. For about a month prior to the trip, they were shown how to milk the cows, take care of the livestock, do the bottling, and make the deliveries to the people in town. Once Dad was satisfied that everything wouldn't fall apart in his absence, we were ready to hit the highway.

It was July 1948 when we loaded Dad's brand new, maroon Ford woody (he bought it only four months before we left) and pulled out of Augusta—heading due south. Route 66, the great highway that connected the Midwest to the West Coast waited for us at the southern tip of the state. We were all excited at the prospect of driving across the country.

For the first portion of the journey, my mother had packed sandwiches, home-baked cookies, and other foods to eat as we wound through the backroads. After we joined up with Highway 66, roadside stands and restaurants were so plentiful that we soon switched to other foods. When the family got hungry, we just stopped in the little towns along the way and bought meals. For Mom, this was a real vacation from the kitchen!

As far as I can remember, Dad always ordered the chicken fried steak. The boys had more variety, including chili and, one of my favorites, hot roast beef sandwiches. In the mornings, it was the standard breakfast: eggs with biscuits and gravy on the side. Other times, my brothers and I filled up on soda pop and candy. Grapette was our favorite Route 66 flavor!

When we weren't stopping to eat or visit the bathroom, my mom dreamed up games for us to play. As we came upon Burma-Shave signs, the first to see them would get the privilege of reading them out loud! Other times, we enjoyed identifying the cars we saw, calling out the colors, and counting how many Indians we encountered. Mom would always have some sort of reward for the "winner" of these motoring pastimes. Usually, it was a dime we could use to buy goodies at the next filling station. For such a long trip, Mom did a tremendous job of keeping us all busy.

My favorite car game was counting horses. We all knew that when we got to California we were going to get to see Roy Rogers and Trigger. For us, it was a big thing because

we watched their exploits nearly every Saturday night at our local movie theater.

To sleep, we stopped at little auto courts—the kind where one could pull the car right in beside the room. We always got two beds: Mom and Dad slept in one, the three boys in the other. Before continuing the next day, we got some time to play around outside and let off a little steam before we climbed into the crowded car and drove back onto 66.

When we reached Arizona, Dad took a little side trip up to the Boulder Dam. When we got there, it was so big that Dad refused to go down into the dam! We were eager to see it, however, and without hesitation went down on the elevator. We were impressed by the massive turbines and the rushing water. It really got our attention, and we've been talking about it ever since. On the way back

In 1948, Clare Patterson, Sr., drove the entire Patterson clan in his brand new Ford Woody to see the sights at the Boulder Dam. Taking a vacation from their Augusta, Kansas, dairy farm, they headed to Van Nuys, California, by way of Route 66. Although his dad decided not to accompany the family down into the dam to see the sights, Clare, Jr., remembers the road trip as one of the best vacations of his life. *Photos courtesy Clare Patterson*

to Kingman and the highway, we stopped at a filling station where Dad gave us some nickels to play the slot machines!

From what I can remember, we went through the desert early in the morning, and it didn't seem that hot to us. We just opened up the windows—I guess we didn't know any better.

What really stands out above the heat was the fun we had in the car: On parts of the highway in the Southwest, the roadbed sometimes followed the contour of the land. As we went over the tiny dips and hills, my dad started to inch down the gas pedal and soon we were flying up and down. We kept yelling "faster, faster" as my Mom warned "you better slow down, you better slow down!" It was one of the best thrills we had along the trip!

When we finally arrived in California, we headed to the city of Van Nuys which at that time, was in the outskirts of Los Angeles. For fun, Mom and Dad took us to Pacific Ocean Park. It was the first time that any of us were around seafood so we decided to sample some of the fare. Unfortunately, my dad and I had a bad reaction to lobster and we both became ill. But that wasn't the most exciting part. We got to ride a real roller-coaster (that went out over the ocean) which made our fun and games along the highway pale in comparison. I had such a great time that I had to do it again, marking the high point of one of my family's greatest adventures. Without a doubt, that summer trip in 1948 was, and always will be, my most memorable trip along Route 66.

—Clare Patterson, Jr.

Crossroads of America

In the 1920s and 1930s, we called my home town of Sapulpa, Oklahoma, "The Crossroads of America." Highway 66 went right down our Main Street and the main north-south route, Highway 75, intersected 66 in the center of town. Highway 75 went from South Texas all the way into Canada.

In 1927, I traveled with my parents and two brothers along Highway 66 from Sapulpa to Los Angeles, California. We had a Hudson touring car and all our camping equipment. It was quite an experience for a five-year-old girl.

One of the more troublesome things on that trip was that the highway was not marked going through towns and cities. One had to keep stopping and asking how to find 66 on the other side of town.

We had a lot of rain on that trip. I remember this because the Hudson's windshield wiper was not electric, thus the person sitting next to the driver had to operate the wiper manually. Also, there were no windows as such, and each time a rain started, there was a mad scramble to get the side curtains out and installed. Much of the highway was not paved, and in June 1927, some of it was underwater. Fortunately, someone had placed poles along each side of the road so that you could see where the roadway was. Cars stuck in deep mud had to be pulled out by mules or tractors.

Whenever we stopped to camp, if we saw another car with Oklahoma license plates, it was like old-home week. We quickly learned that if we left our campsite to visit nearby points of interest, such as the Petrified Forest, Meteor Crater, or the Grand Canyon, wild creatures up to and including bears were quite likely to vandalize the camping area in search of our "grub box."

We had many flat tires and several broken fan belts. My father and brothers had quite a time changing and patching all those tires. When we needed a fan belt, one of my brothers would hitchhike to the nearest town to get one and then catch a ride back.

Mountain roads at that time were one lane only. If we were unlucky enough to meet another car, either they or we would

Rebecca Rockwood Hill (at age five) camping with her father and two brothers near Flagstaff, Arizona. Though not evident in this photograph, her mother is most likely off somewhere performing duties related to the preparation of food. The Hudson touring car parked to the right of the tent is loaded down with spare tires. *Photos courtesy Rebecca Rockwood Hill*

have to back up to the nearest turnout to let the other car pass. On one occasion, we met a woman who refused to back up. Many angry words were exchanged. It was only a short distance for her to backup to a turnout, but my father finally had to backup quite a long distance so that we could let her pass.

When we finally reached the Pacific coast, we treated ourselves to a nice motel on the beach—such a luxury after all that camping and cooking under difficult circumstances.

—Rebecca Rockwood Hill

California Bound in Ford's Flivver

My parents, Harry and Grace Richards, departed the town of Summersville, Missouri, in the spring of 1919 for a road trip across America. At the time, I was 18 years old and my sister, Carol, only eight. It was no leisure trip: we were moving to the West and driving all the way. San Dimas, California, was our final destination, one we would reach by motorcar in an age long before there were any hard-surfaced roads, multi-lane freeways, or even a Route 66.

The arduous journey that lay ahead promised to be an adventure of a lifetime and on that account, it did not fail to disappoint. Seventy-seven years have passed since that eventful trek, but the memories still replay in my mind as vividly as if they had happened yesterday.

My mom and dad didn't have a fancy phaeton or any type of trailer, but they did own a simple Model T Ford Touring Car that featured "isinglass" side curtains. Its running boards were used to store things, and a utility trunk strapped on the back housed all of our food and supplies. Inside, Dad toted a round, coal oil (kerosene) stove, which we used for extra heat at night. Space was limited on board, so each of us were allowed to bring only one suitcase—four in total, the youngest member of our clan bringing along a "keyster"(suitcase made of straw)!

In those early days of motor travel, things taken for granted today didn't even exist. The going was really rough out there between the large towns. Between towns, there were no filling stations or amenities of any kind to be found—no fast-food service, no campsites with electricity, and definitely no motels in this final year of the teens. This made for some very exciting times and dictated that three very special tanks had to be kept full at all times. One was a gasoline canister, another an oil container, and the third a large canvas bag filled to the brim with water (it hung from the radiator and had to be refilled without fail daily). These reserve supplies were our own special form of trip insurance!

For food, we usually ate meals at truckers' stops or other places in towns. This was only once in a while, so most of our "dinners" consisted of cold lunches and other foods we could easily carry with us. My parents purchased fruit and other snacks that were eaten along the way, and I remember that I ate enough cheese and crackers to last a lifetime! Of course, Dad always started the day by filling his Thermos full of coffee, something the

When she was 18 years old, Mabel Richards Phillips (second from the left) made the trip across America long before there were any hard-surfaced roads, multilane freeways, or even a Route 66 to speak of. Her mother, Grace (left), sister, Carol, and father, Harry, accompanied her on the trip from Summersville, Missouri to San Dimas, California. *Photos courtesy Mabel Richards Phillips*

rest of the family members did not drink. I guess he needed the extra energy considering all the responsibilities of the journey.

When we reached Oklahoma by means of the Old Wire Road—the rough pathway that later became the Ozark Trail and even later part of Route 66—we met a couple of young men by the names of Vance and Henry who were also venturing by automobile out to the West Coast. We struck up a conversation, and it didn't take long for the pair to ask us if they could follow us. After all, we were all going the same way and in those days, everyone helped each other while crossing the country by car. Vehicles often formed a kind of caravan, much like the old wagon trains of the pioneer days. That way, everyone

wasn't so alone in the remote wilderness and we could count on one another for obtaining help during times of trouble or mechanical breakdown. Besides, it also created a certain camaraderie that buoyed our spirits throughout the treacherous journey into the unknown territories of the West.

We routinely spent the nights under the open skies, since hotels in towns were usually extravagant affairs that were too expensive with rooms too fancy for a dust-covered family on a tight travel budget. Nevertheless, we always found a place to stay along the trails, often bunking down in deserted houses, quiet school yards, or any other place along the roadside that looked like it had a large enough clearing to set up our

A circa-1911 truck crosses the Colorado River by ferry between Arizona and California at Ehrenburg Scow, pushed by a power boat ferry. Fortunately, modern bridges made this precarious crossing considerably easier once Highway 66 was paved from end to end. A.L. Westgard photo, 1911. *National Archives*

tent. When possible, we even gathered up tumbleweeds and newspapers so that we could insulate our cots at night to stave off the high winds and low temperatures. Of course, public bathroom facilities were non-existent in those days, and we had to make do with what nature provided.

Because of the open design of our modest family flivver, the weather often posed considerable problems for us on the journey. In the prairies of Kansas, we experienced such strong winds that seeing the highway through the blowing dust and dirt was almost impossible. When it rained, driving was difficult at best—windshield wipers were not a feature of the simple Ford. After a long deluge, the dirt roads that we traveled became nothing more than

muddy ruts. As a result, my parents' biggest fear was bogging down in the mud with no way to get out. Near larger towns, teams of horses were often used to haul stuck vehicles out of mud traps. In remote regions, however, there was often no assistance available. One had to rely on their wits and ingenuity, of which I learned my parents had a considerable amount.

At one point during this great overland journey, things were feeling pretty crowded in the small compartment of our Model T, so the two young men we met offered to take little Carol in their car for a while. It sounded like a great idea to everyone, except that she ended up crying for her mother so much that the boys wondered if they had done the right thing. Mother Grace was so concerned about not seeing Carol that she carried on as well. It only took one day of that to reunite our small family in a common vehicle!

Not surprisingly, these personal problems were the least of my father's worries. As pilot, mechanic, and navigator, the trip was rife with all sorts of difficulties and concerns for him. It was slow going, with little mileage accumulated. Flat tires had to be dealt with on a continual basis, and my father always had the same thought in the back of his mind, "just where are we going to get our next tank of gasoline?" Oil and water were an important commodity as well—but of secondary ranking when the fuel tank appeared to be down to its last drop. Antifreeze was unheard of, so in the mountainous regions along the way, my father had to actually drain the entire radiator of its fluid so that during the frigid nights the cooling system would not freeze up and crack the engine block.

In New Mexico, we were looking for a place to sleep when father got a tip from some people to drive up an old dirt road and look for an abandoned miner's cabin. The "road" was very difficult to cross and led us high into the hills. Around that time, the worst possible thing that could happen did: the old Ford started acting up and making really strange noises. The radiator needed water and we were all out, so my dad drove across a very bumpy field where he spied a small herd of cattle huddled around a windmill. Unfortunately, the water in the small stock tank we came upon was frozen solid. Undaunted, Dad retrieved a hand-held hatchet from the tool box and started to chop up the ice layer. Using the trusty old canvas water bag, he scooped up a bagful of frigid water and refilled the radiator. We were back on our way.

When we finally reached the border of Arizona, the dirt trace dubbed the National Old Trails Road came right up to the great Colorado River and stopped! It wasn't until then that we learned there were no bridges to be crossed. The only way to get our automobile to the other side was to drive onto a rickety old ferry that didn't look like it could support its own weight much less the heft of our fully loaded rig. Still, there were no other practical means to ford the water, so we had to swallow our fears and brave the rushing waters. Amazingly, we managed to get across without incident.

Looking back from today's perspective and 95 years of living, it seems amazing that we made it safe and sound across the country to California without any major mishap. It was a big accomplishment, since the roads we traveled on were nothing more than blazed trails—youngsters who would later grow to become the smooth concrete roads with official-sounding names such as Highway 66. In 1919, we endured hardships and made sacrifices that today's traveler would never dream of. Still, my parents' old Model T was a hardy machine; it got us all the way to a new life in California, put a little adventure into all our lives, and kicked up quite a bit of dust along the way. And that my friends, is what traveling across country is all about.

—Mabel Richards Phillips

Hicksatomic is one of the smaller Illinois gasoline marketers that faded into obscurity. Today, reminders of the diverse selection of gas brands existing just 20 years ago are all that are left along Highway 66. Wilmington, Illinois. *D. Jeanene Tiner ©1995*

Epilogue

Route 66: Memories of a Forgotten Highway

A Tribute to Jack Kerouac

What does one remember of Route 66? Is it the sound of the tires as they hum along the pavement? The whine of an engine straining to top a hill? Is it the pictures of street signs flashing past like so many frames in a nickelodeon?

Perhaps it's the conversation of the road or the songs heard on the radio—the sounds broadcast from unfamiliar towns and mysterious disc jockeys howling in the western night. Could it be the look of excitement in a child's eyes or that feeling of joy experienced when crossing a state line or making one's mileage goal before dusk? It could very well be all of these.

For some, it's the service stations and the gasoline they provide, the smell of evaporating motor fuel, the fragrance of burning oil, and the ammonia of windshield cleaning spray as the attendant wipes the windows. It's the cold soda pop pulled from an icy machine and the simple pleasure of popping the top on a machine-mounted bottle opener while a gas pump rings and the hood slams down. It's visions of fan belts, car parts, and gadgets seen through the plate glass window of the station office, the idle curiosity about what these people do when they close down at night. Where do all these people go after a day of dedication to the road and the stream of travelers that anonymously patronize their businesses?

Route 66 is also the meals eaten along the way, and the amazing variety offered the palate. It's the candy bar gobbled in the front seat, or even a chunk of Spam wrenched right from the can with an old pocket knife, after driving for endless hours with no food in your stomach. It's the taste of a simple sandwich lovingly slathered with deviled ham by your wife, mom, or grandma—wrapped in wax paper and stacked like bricks in your cooler—and washed down with chilled water chugged from a collapsible drinking cup. It's the thick diesel-and-bacon smell of a truck stop.

It's the indelible impression made by a cheap hamburger and French fry combination—the homemade kind—complete with all the grease and trimmings that

Far from the hurried climate of the interstate highways, the "free road" routinely offers up the unexpected. Along the quiet miles of cracked asphalt, travelers may experience the wonders often missed. Life in the "slow lane" has its advantages over an addiction to cruise control. Between Miami and Afton, Oklahoma. *Shellee Graham ©1995*

always drip down your chin and get the seats all messy no matter how careful you are and how many napkins you have handy. It's the friendly service of a gum-smacking, drawling waitress with a little apron and cat's-eye glasses—the "ya'll come back now" as you head out the door with a stomach full of grits and gravy.

It's the tasty memories of home-fried chicken just like mama used to make, the barbecue, the pan-fried river trout, the broiled rabbit, and the handmade tortillas formed and fried right before your eyes as an old woman

all-you-can-eat frenzy of the dinnertime traveler's buffet.

When the stomach is full and the food forgotten, Route 66 is the amazing sights encountered along the road-side and all the wonder of our weird, wild America. It's gigantic dinosaurs, drive-in restaurants adorned with swooping neon, unexplained phenomenon, and sad and crazy shrines to human indi-viduality—like giant balls of twine or the world's largest bundle of barbed wire—dis-played with the sole intention of causing the tourist to stand back and utter "wow!"

It's the vivid images of a snake handler as he thrusts his pole into a cage and pulls out a gigantic rat-tler ready to strike. It's the wriggling wonder of an alligator paraded in front of the public like some freak of nature, and the home-made "museum" featuring a two-headed goat pre-served in formaldehyde displayed right next to a stuffed javelina with glass eyes and horrible teeth scar-ing little children and providing your subconscious with nightmare fodder for years to come.

It's the rubber Indian hatchet or cheap, imitation moc-casins—made in Japan—that were purchased in the adjoin-ing trading post that was open 24 hours for customer con-venience. It's watching the throngs of tourists, dressed in loud, patterned bowling shirts and print tunics with poly-ester pants and bolo ties, drinking in the sights and sounds

in the back hand-grinds corn meal just like her ancestors have for the past 500 years.

It's how cool and tasty the water was and "wasn't that just about the best tasting iced-tea we ever drank?" It's the sizzle that remains in the mind long after the steak is digested and the memories of what the town even looked like disintegrate into thin air.

It's the lobster bibs that you have to wear just to eat some seafood in a joint that tries real hard to be classy despite the glittery vinyl upholstery and the cheap table candles with fish-net coverings to set the mood. It's even the cockroach that waltzes boldly across your table that no one notices or cares about as much as the plates piled high with vittles from the they can't see at home—all the while their pocket Instamatic cameras clicking and whirring.

For all motorists, Route 66 is driving all day and then finding a tourist court that looks cozy and inviting, its "vacancy" sign drawing the motorist to its hearth—a genuinely friendly and homey place that really does invite the road weary to "just stop and rest a while." It's an Indian wigwam one can actually sleep in when the time comes to turn out the light and wait for the moon to make its arc across the night sky.

It's the secure feeling of knowing your car is parked right outside your room and that the desk clerk really does care "if you need anything." Its the friendly attitude of the maid who lives in her own cabin right out back. It's all part of the experience, including the television that only receives two fuzzy channels, the threadbare pillowcases, and the bedspread that hasn't been laundered since Roosevelt held office.

It's the telephone with the rotary dialer and the inability to access long-distance without the operator listening in on your calls. It's the shower curtain that sticks to your body as you try to take a bath and the few postage-stamp-sized towels available to dry yourself off.

In the final analysis, what's really remembered of Route 66 are those small towns and bustling main streets, the filling stations, the tourist courts and ramshackle roadside cabins, strange attractions, the endless parade of curio shops, the restaurants, the greasy spoons, the diners, the ice cream stands, the drive-in theaters, and a myriad of other wonders that make it worthwhile to hop in a car in downtown Chicago and roll over the great groaning continent to meet the sun-drenched shores of the Pacific. The beginning of a journey and the point of arrival are often just that: the beginning and end. Real memories—and life itself—are made up of all the sights, smells, sounds, and tastes along the way. Events that can only be experienced . . . on the road.

—Michael Karl Witzel, the Texas Hill Country, 1996

Lester Dill acquired ownership of Meramec Caverns in the early 1930s and turned the cave into a well-known Route 66 landmark. Newspapers in St. Louis described Dill as a "self-styled caveologist, promoter of the P.T. Barnum school and a quiet benefactor of both causes and persons in need." Through an unabashed campaign of promotion and highway publicity (he once touted the caves as Jesse James' hideout), he developed a natural wonder and made it into a much-loved tourist destination now remembered as a Mother Road favorite. His numerous barn paintings that advertised the caverns ("See Meramec Caverns, Route 66 Mo.") rose to become almost as famous as the signs of Burma Shave. Today, the caves are still a vital part of the Route 66 legacy. Near the Meramec River, Stanton, Missouri. *Courtesy Jerry Keyser*

Recommended Two-Lane Reading

Anderson, Warren H. *Vanishing Roadside America*. Tucson: The University of Arizona Press, 1981.

Andrews, J.J.C. *The Well-Built Elephant and Other Roadside Attractions: A Tribute to American Eccentricity*. New York: Congdon & Weed, Inc., 1984.

Baeder, John. *Gas, Food, and Lodging: A Postcard Odyssey Through the Great American Roadside*. New York: Abbeville Press, 1982.

Belasco, Warren James. *Americans on the Road: From Autocamp to Motel, 1910–1945*. Cambridge, Massachusetts: M.I.T. Press, 1979.

Blake, Peter. *God's Own Junkyard: The Planned Deterioration of America's Landscape*. New York: Holt, Rinehart and Winston, 1964.

Boyne, Walter J. *Power Behind the Wheel: Creativity and Evolution of the Automobile*. New York: Stewart, Tabori & Chang, 1988.

Buckley, Patricia. *Route 66: Remnants*. Arizona: Historic Route 66 Association of Arizona, 1989.

Butler, John L. *First Highways of America*. Iola, Wisconsin: Krause Publications, 1994.

Clark, Marian. *The Route 66 Cook Book*. Tulsa, Oklahoma: Council Oaks Books, 1993.

Crump, Spencer. *Route 66: America's First Main Street*. Corona Del Mar, California: Zeta Publishers, 1994.

Curtis, C.H. *The Missouri U.S. 66 Tour Book*. St. Louis, Missouri: Curtis Enterprises, 1994.

Davies, Vivian, and Darin Kuna. *Guide to Historic Route 66 in California*. LaVerne, California: California Route 66 Association, 1993.

Finch, Christopher. *Highways to Heaven: The Auto Biography of America*. New York: HarperCollins Publishers, Inc., 1992.

Flink, James J. *The Automobile Age*. Cambridge, Massachusetts: M.I.T. Press, 1988.

Hart, Virginia. *The Story of American Roads*. New York: William Sloan Association, 1950.

Heat Moon, William Least. *Blue Highways: A Journey Into America*. Boston: Atlantic Monthly Press, 1982.

Heimann, Jim, and Rip Georges. *California Crazy: Roadside Vernacular Architecture*. San Francisco: Chronicle Books, 1980.

Hess, Alan. *Googie: 1950s Coffee Shop Architecture*. San Francisco: Chronicle Books, 1985.

Hilleson, K. *Route 66 Revisited: A Wanderer's Guide to New Mexico—Volume 2: Albuquerque to the Arizona Border*. Albuquerque, New Mexico: Nakii Enterprises, 1988.

Keller, Ulrich. *The Highway as Habitat: A Roy Stryker Documentation, 1943–1955*. Santa Barbara, California: University Art Museum, 1986.

Kerouac, Jack. *On the Road*. New York: Viking Penguin, 1955.

Kurtz, Stephen A. *Wasteland: Building the American Dream*. New York: Praeger Publishers, 1973.

Langdon, Philip. *Orange Roofs, Golden Arches: The Architecture of American Chain Restaurants*. New York: Alfred A. Knopf, 1986.

Leavitt, Helen. *Superhighways Superhoax*. New York: Doubleday, 1970.

Leverton, Bill. *On the Arizona Road*. Phoenix, Arizona: Golden West Publishers, 1986.

Lewis, David L., and Lawrence Goldstein. *The Automobile and American Culture*. Ann Arbor: The University of Michigan Press, 1980.

Liebs, Chester. *Main Street to Miracle Mile: American Roadside Architecture*. Boston: Little, Brown & Co., 1985.

Marling, Karal Ann. *The Colossus of Roads: Myth and Symbol Along the American Highway*. Minneapolis: University of Minnesota Press, 1984.

Moore, Bob, and Patrick Grauwels. *A Guidebook to the Mother Road*. Del Mar, California: USDC, Inc., 1994.

Noe, Sally. *66 Sights on Route 66*. Gallup, New Mexico: Gallup Downtown Development Group, 1992.

Patton, Phil. *Open Road: A Celebration of the American Highway*. New York: Simon & Schuster, 1986.

Phillips Petroleum Co. *Phillips: The First 66 Years*. Edited by William C. Wertz. A public affairs publication of Phillips Petroleum Co., 1983.

Rittenhouse, Jack D. *A Guide Book to Highway 66*. Albuquerque, New Mexico: University of New Mexico Press, 1989. (Reprint of 1946 issue).

Rose, Albert C. *Historic American Roads: From Frontier Trails to Superhighways*. New York: Crown Publishers, 1976.

Ross, Jim. *Oklahoma Route 66: The Cruiser's Companion*. Bethany, Oklahoma: Ghost Town Press, 1992.

Ross, Jim, with art by Jerry McClanahan. *Route 66: The Map Series*. Bethany, Oklahoma: Ghost Town Press, 1994.

Rowsome, Frank, Jr. *The Verse by the Side of the Road*. New York: The Stephen Greene Press/Pelham Books, 1990.

Schneider, Jill. *Route 66 Across New Mexico: A Wanderer's Guide*. Albuquerque, New Mexico: University of New Mexico Press, 1991.

Scott, Quinta, and Susan Croce Kelly. *Route 66: The Highway and its People*. Norman, Oklahoma: University of Oklahoma Press, 1988.

Silk, Gerald, Angelo Anselmi, Henry Robert, Jr., and Strother MacMinn. *Automobile and Culture*. New York: Harry N. Abrams, Inc., 1984.

Snyder, Tom. *The Route 66 Traveler's Companion*. New York: St. Martin's Press, 1990.

Society for Commercial Archeology. *The Automobile in Design and Culture*. Edited by Jan Jennings. Ames: Iowa State University Press, 1990.

Steinbeck, John. *The Grapes of Wrath*. New York: Viking Press, 1939.

Steinbeck, John. *Travels with Charley*. New York: Viking Press, 1962.

Stern, Jane, and Michael Stern. *RoadFood*. New York: HarperCollins Publishers, Inc., 1992.

Teague, Thomas. *Searching for 66*. Springfield, Illinois: Samizdat House, 1991.

Wallis, Michael. *Route 66: The Mother Road*. New York: St. Martin's Press, 1990.

Wallis, Michael, and Suzanne Fitzgerald Wallis. *Route 66 Postcards*. New York: St. Martin's Press, 1993.

Wilkins, Mike, Ken Smith, and Doug Kirby. *The New Roadside America*. New York: Simon & Schuster, 1992.

Witzel, Michael. *The American Gas Station: History and Folklore of the Gas Station in American Car Culture*. Osceola, Wisconsin: Motorbooks International, 1992.

Witzel, Michael. *The American Drive-In: History and Folklore of the Drive-In Restaurant in American Car Culture*. Osceola, Wisconsin: Motorbooks International, 1994.

Witzel, Michael. *Gas Station Memories*. Osceola, Wisconsin: Motorbooks International, 1994.

Index